SPACES OF GLOBAL CAPITALISM

CONTENTS

INTRODUCTION

Introduction:
Hettner-Lecture 2004 in Heidelberg

Peter Meusburger and Hans Gebhardt

The Department of Geography, University of Heidelberg, held its eighth 'Hettner-Lecture' from June 28 to July 2, 2004. This annual lecture series, named after Alfred Hettner, Professor of Geography in Heidelberg from 1899 to 1928 and one of the most reputable German geographers of his day, is devoted to new theoretical developments in the crossover fields of geography, economics, the social sciences, and the humanities.

During their stay, the invited guest-speakers present two public lectures, one of which is transmitted via teleteaching on the Internet. In addition, several seminars give graduate students and young researchers the opportunity to meet and converse with an internationally acclaimed scholar. Such an experience at an early stage in the academic career opens up new perspectives for research and encourages critical reflection on current theoretical debates and geographical practice.

The eighth Hettner-Lecture was given by David Harvey, Distinguished Professor of Anthropology at the City University of New York Graduate Center. David Harvey is widely recognized as one of the most innovative and influential geographical thinkers of the last 40 years. His *Explanation in geography* (1969) provided a major contribution to the methodological debate over geography as a spatial science that captivated geographers in the 1960s. Harvey's subsequent move from the UK – where he had lectured at Bristol University – to the Johns Hopkins University in Baltimore coincided with a profound shift in the intellectual foundations of his research. With *Social justice and the city* (1973), Harvey produced a pioneering text in critical urban studies that explored the relevance of Marxist ways of thinking to account for and challenge poverty and racism in Western cities. His *The limits to capital* (1982), a geographical extension of Marx's theory of capitalism, firmly established Harvey as leading Marxist geographer with his reputation extending well beyond the confines of the discipline. Harvey returned to urban issues in *The urbanization of capital* (1985) and *Consciousness and the urban experience* (1985), before embarking on his most successful book to date, *The condition of postmodernity* (1989), a materialist critique of postmodernism written while he held the Halford Mackinder Chair in Geography at the University of Oxford. More recently, Harvey has revisited and further explored issues of social justice and the idea of utopia in *Justice, nature and the geography of difference* (1996) and *Spaces of hope* (2000). His latest books are *Paris, capital of modernity* (2003) and *The new imperialism* (2003).

During the Hettner-Lecture 2004 David Harvey presented two public lectures entitled 'Free market capitalism and the restoration of class power' and 'Towards a general theory of uneven geographical development',[1] both of which are published here in revised form, together with an essay on 'Space as a key word' and a short photographic documentation. Three seminars with graduate students and young researchers from Heidelberg and nineteen other European and US universities took up issues raised in the lectures. The seminars were entitled 'The new imperialism', 'Geographical knowledges/political powers', and 'Space as a key word'.

We should like to express our gratitude to the *Klaus Tschira Foundation* for generously supporting the Hettner-Lecture. Particular

---

1. 'Free Market Capitalism and the Restoration of Class Power', *Alte Aula der Universität*, Monday, June 28, 2004, 18.15; afterwards reception. 'Towards a general theory of uneven geographical development', *Hörsaal des Geographischen Instituts*, Tuesday, June 29, 2004, 15.15. The second lecture was followed by a public discussion, chaired by Michael Hoyler (Loughborough).

thanks are due to Dr. h.c. Klaus Tschira, our benevolent host in the *Studio* of the foundation's magnificent *Villa Bosch*. We would like to thank Prof. Dr. Angelos Chaniotis, Vice-Rector of Heidelberg University, and Prof. Dr. Peter Hofmann, Dean of the Faculty of Chemistry and Earth Sciences, for their welcome addresses at the opening ceremony in the university's *Alte Aula*.

The Hettner-Lecture 2004 would not have been possible without the full commitment of all involved students and faculty members. We thank Tim Freytag and Heike Jöns for their effective organisational work and the planning and chairing of the seminar sessions with graduate students and young researchers. We are also grateful to the students who helped with the organisation of the event. The concerted effort and enthusiasm of all participants once more ensured a successful Hettner-Lecture in Heidelberg.

NEO-LIBERALISM AND THE RESTORATION OF CLASS POWER

Neo-liberalism and the restoration of class power

David Harvey

President Bush repeatedly asserts that the US has conferred the precious gift of "freedom" on the Iraqi people. "Freedom," he says, "is the Almighty's gift to every man and woman in this world" and "as the greatest power on earth we have an obligation to help the spread of freedom."[1] This official mantra (repeatedly advanced by the administration and the military) that the supreme achievement of the pre-emptive invasion of Iraq has been to render the country "free" is echoed throughout much of the media in the US and appears to be a persuasive argument for many to continue to support the war even though the official reasons given for it (such as connections between Saddam and al-Qaeda, the existence of weapons of mass destruction and direct threats to US security) have been found wanting. Freedom, however, is a tricky word. As Matthew Arnold observed many years ago: "freedom is a very good horse to ride, but to ride somewhere."[2] To what destination, then, are the Iraqi people expected to ride the horse of freedom so generously donated to them?

The US answer to this question was spelled out on September 19,

---

1. G.W. Bush, "President Addresses the Nation in Prime Time Press Conference," April 13th, 2004; http://www.whitehouse.gov/news/releases/2004/04/20040413–20.html.
2. Matthew Arnold is cited in R. Williams, *Culture and Society, 1780–1850* (London: Chatto and Windus, 1958), p. 118.

2003, when Paul Bremer, head of the Coalition Provisional Authority, promulgated orders that included "the full privatization of public enterprises, full ownership rights by foreign firms of Iraqi businesses, full repatriation of foreign profits . . . the opening of Iraq's banks to foreign control, national treatment for foreign companies and . . . the elimination of nearly all trade barriers."[3] The orders were to apply to all arenas of the economy, including public services, the media, manufacturing, services, transportation, finance, and construction. Only oil was exempt (presumably because of its special status and geopolitical significance as a weapon of distinctively US control). The right to unionize and to strike, on the other hand, were strictly circumscribed. A highly regressive "flat tax" (an ambition long held by the US conservatives) was also imposed. These orders were, as Naomi Klein points out, in violation of the Geneva and Hague Conventions since an occupying power is mandated to guard the assets of an occupied country and has no right to sell them off.[4] There is, furthermore, considerable resistance to the imposition of what the London *Economist* calls a "capitalist dream" upon Iraq. Even Iraq's interim trade minister, a US appointed member of the Coalition Provisional Authority, attacked the forced imposition of "free market fundamentalism," describing it as "a flawed logic that ignores history."[5] Almost certainly, as Klein also points out, the initial US resistance to direct elections in Iraq stemmed from its desire to work with appointed representatives who would be as pliant as possible in locking in these free-market reforms before direct democracy (which would almost certainly reject them) took over. While Bremer's rules would be judged illegal if imposed by an occupying power, they would likely be considered legal under international law if confirmed by a "sovereign" (even if unelected and interim) government. The interim government that took over at the end of June 2004, though dubbed "sovereign," only had

3. A. Juhasz, "Ambitions of Empire: the Bush Administration Economic Plan for Iraq (and Beyond)," *LeftTurn Magazine*, No.12 Feb/March 2004.
4. N. Klein, "Of course the White House fears free elections in Iraq," *The Guardian*, January 24, 2004, p. 18.
5. T. Crampton, "Iraqi official urges caution on imposing free market," *New York Times*, October 14, 2003, C5.

the power to confirm existing laws. It could not modify existing laws or write new ones (though given the personnel involved it was unlikely that it would have departed radically from the Bremer decrees).

The neo-liberal turn

What the US evidently seeks to impose by main force on Iraq is a full-fledged neo-liberal state apparatus whose fundamental mission is to facilitate conditions for profitable capital accumulation. The sorts of measures that Bremer outlined, according to neo-liberal theory, are both necessary and sufficient for the creation of wealth and therefore for the improved well-being of whole populations. The conflation of political freedom with freedom of the market and of trade has long been a cardinal feature of neo-liberal policy and it has dominated the US stance towards the rest of the world for many years. On the first anniversary of 9/11, for example, President Bush announced in an op-ed piece published in the *New York Times*, that "We will use our position of unparalleled strength and influence to build an atmosphere of international order and openness in which progress and liberty can flourish in many nations. A peaceful world of growing freedom serves American long-term interests, reflects enduring American ideals and unites America's allies . . . We seek a just peace where repression, resentment and poverty are replaced with the hope of democracy, development, free markets and free trade," these last two having "proved their ability to lift whole societies out of poverty." Today, he concluded, "humanity holds in its hands the opportunity to offer freedom's triumph over all its age-old foes. The United States welcomes its responsibility to lead in this great mission." This same language appeared in the prologue to the National Defense Strategy Document published shortly thereafter.[6] It is this freedom, interpreted as freedom of the market and of trade, that is to be imposed upon Iraq and the world.

---

6. G.W. Bush, "Securing Freedom's Triumph," *New York Times*, September 11th, 2002, p. A33. *The National Security Strategy of the United State of America* can be found on the website: www.whitehouse.gov/nsc/nss.html.

It is useful to recall here, that the first great experiment with neo-
liberal state formation was Chile after Pinochet's coup on the "little
September 11th" of 1973 (almost thirty years to the day before Bremer's
announcement of the regime to be installed in Iraq). The coup, against
the democratically-elected and leftist social democratic government of
Salvador Allende, was strongly backed by the CIA and supported by US
Secretary of State Henry Kissinger. It violently repressed all the social
movements and political organization of the left and dismantled all
forms of popular organization (such as the community health centers in
poorer neighborhoods). The labor market was "freed" from regulatory
or institutional restraints (trade union power, for example). But by 1973
the policies of import substitution that had formerly dominated in Latin
American attempts at economic regeneration (and which had succeeded
to some degree in Brazil after the military coup of 1964) had fallen into
disrepute. With the world economy in the midst of a serious recession,
something new was plainly called for. A group of economists known as
"the Chicago boys," because of their attachment to the theories of
Milton Friedman then teaching at the University of Chicago, were
summoned to help reconstruct the Chilean economy. They did so
along free-market lines, privatizing public assets, opening up natural
resources to private exploitation and facilitating foreign direct investment and free trade. The right of foreign companies to repatriate profits
from their Chilean operations was guaranteed. Export-led growth was
favored over import substitution. The only sector reserved for the state
was the key resource of copper (rather like oil in Iraq). The subsequent
short-term revival of the Chilean economy in terms of growth rates,
capital accumulation, and high rates of return on foreign investments,
provided evidence upon which the subsequent turn to more open neo-
liberal policies in both Britain (under Thatcher) and the US (under
Reagan) could be modeled. Not for the first time, a brutal experiment
carried out in the periphery became a model for the formulation of
policies in the center (much as experimentation with the flat tax in Iraq
is now proposed).[7]

7. J. Valdez, *Pinochet's Economists: The Chicago School in Chile* (New York:
   Cambridge University Press, 1995).

The Chilean experiment demonstrated, however, that the benefits were not well-distributed. The country and its ruling elites along with foreign investors did well enough while the people in general fared badly. This has been a persistent enough effect of neo-liberal policies over time as to be regarded as structural to the whole project. Dumenil and Levy go so far as to argue that neo-liberalism was from the very beginning a project to achieve the restoration of class power to the richest strata in the population. Commenting on how the top one percent of income earners in the US fared, they write:

> Before World War II, these households received about 16 percent of total income. This percentage fell rapidly during the war and, in the 1960s, it had been reduced to 8 percent, a plateau which was maintained during three decades. In the mid 1980s, it soared suddenly and by the end of the century it reached 15 percent. Looking at total wealth, the trend is broadly identical . . .[8]

Other data show that the top 0.1 percent of income earners increased their share of the national income from 2 percent in 1978 to over 6 percent by 1999. Almost certainly, with the Bush administration's tax cuts now taking effect, the concentration of wealth in the upper echelons of society is continuing a-pace. Dumenil and Levy also noted that "the structural crisis of the 1970s, with rates of interest hardly superior to inflation rates, low dividend payout by corporations, and depressed stock markets, further encroached on the income and wealth of the wealthiest" during those years. Not only were the 1970s characterized by a global crisis of stagflation, but this was the period when the power of the upper classes was most seriously threatened. Neo-liberalism arose, the argument goes, as a response to this threat.[9]

But substantiation of this thesis of restoration of class power requires that we identify a specific constellation of class forces assembled behind the turn to neo-liberal policies since in neither Britain nor the United

8. G. Duménil and D. Lévy, "Neo-Liberal Dynamics: A New Phase?" Unpublished MS, 2004, p. 4. See also "Task Force on Inequality and American Democracy", *American Democracy in an Age of Rising Inequality* (American Political Science Association, 2004) p. 3.
9. Ibid.

States was it possible to resort to violence of the Chilean sort. It was necessary to construct consent. We must go back to the crucial decade of the 1970s to see how this was done.

The social democratic state in Europe and the Keynesian compromise that grounded the social compact between capital and labor in the US, had worked well enough during the high growth years of the 1950s and 1960s. Redistributive politics, controls over the free mobility of capital, public expenditures and welfare state building had gone hand in hand with relatively high rates of capital accumulation and adequate profitability in most of the advanced capitalist countries. But by the end of the 1960s this began to break down, both internationally and within domestic economies. By 1973, even before the Arab-Israeli War and the OPEC oil embargo, the Bretton Woods system that had regulated international economic relations had dissolved. Signs of a serious crisis of capital accumulation were everywhere apparent, ushering in a global phase of stagflation, fiscal crises of various states (Britain had to be bailed out by the International Monetary Fund in 1975–6 and New York City went technically bankrupt in the same year, while retrenchment in state expenditures was almost everywhere in evidence). The Keynesian compromise had evidently collapsed as a viable way to manage capital accumulation consistent with social democratic politics.[10]

The left answer to this was to deepen state control and regulation of the economy (including, if necessary, curbing the aspirations of labor and popular movements through austerity measures and wage and price controls) without, however, ever challenging head on the powers of capital accumulation. This answer was advanced by socialist and communist parties in alliance in Europe (with hopes pinned on innovative experiments in governance and management of capital accumulation in places like "Red Bologna" or in the turn towards a more open market-socialism and ideas of "eurocommunism" in Italy and Spain). The left assembled considerable popular power behind that program, coming close to power in Italy, actually acquiring state power

10. P. Armstrong, A. Glynn and J. Harrison, *Capitalism Since World War II: The Making and Breaking of the Long Boom* (Oxford: Basil Blackwell, 1991).

in France, Portugal, Spain and Britain and maintaining power in Scandinavia. Even in the United States, a Congress controlled by the Democratic Party legislated a huge wave of regulatory reform (signed into law by Richard Nixon, a Republican President) in the early 1970s governing environmental, labor, consumer and civil rights issues.[11] But broadly the left failed to go much beyond traditional social democratic solutions and these had by the mid-1970s proven inconsistent with the requirements of capital accumulation. The effect was to polarize debate between social democratic forces on the one hand (who were often engaged in a pragmatic politics of curbing the aspirations of their own constituencies) and the interests of all those concerned with re-establishing more open conditions for active capital accumulation on the other.

Neo-liberalism as a potential antidote to threats to the capitalist social order and as a solution to capitalism's ills had long been lurking in the wings of public policy. But it was only during the troubled years of the 1970s that it began to move center stage, particularly in the US and Britain, nurtured in various think tanks such as the Institute for Economic Affairs in London and at the University of Chicago. It gained respectability by the award of the Nobel Prize in economics to two of its leading proponents, von Hayek in 1974 and Milton Friedman in 1976. And it gradually began to exert practical influence. During the Carter presidency, for example, deregulation of the economy emerged as one of the answers to the chronic state of stagflation that had prevailed in the US throughout the 1970s. But the dramatic consolidation of neo-liberalism as a new economic orthodoxy regulating public policy in the advanced capitalist world occurred in the United States and Britain in 1979.

In May of that year Margaret Thatcher was elected in Britain with a strong mandate to reform the economy. Under the influence of the thinking of Keith Joseph and the Institute of Economic Affairs, she accepted that Keynesianism had to be abandoned and that monetarist "supply-side" solutions were essential to cure the stagflation that had characterized the British economy during the 1970s. She recognized

11. Ibid.

that this meant nothing short of a revolution in fiscal and social policies and immediately signaled a fierce determination to have done with the institutions and political ways of the social democratic state that had been consolidated in Britain since 1945. This meant confronting trade union power, attacking all forms of social solidarity (such as those expressed through socialist municipal governance) that hindered competitive flexibility (including the power of many professionals and their associations), dismantling or rolling back the commitments of the welfare state, the privatization of public enterprises (including social housing), reducing taxes, encouraging entrepreneurial initiative and creating a favorable business climate to induce a strong inflow of foreign investment (particularly from Japan).

What Pinochet did through coercive state violence was done by Thatcher through the organization of democratic consent. On this point, Gramsci's observation that consent and hegemony must be organized ahead of revolutionary action – and Thatcher was indeed a self-proclaimed revolutionary – is deeply relevant. Strong currents of thought, willingly propagated through a media that was more and more subservient to the interests of big capital, about individualism, freedom, liberty as opposed to trade union power and stifling bureaucratic ineptitude on the part of the state had become widespread in Britain during the bleak years of economic stagnation during the 1970s. A crisis of capitalism was interpreted as a crisis of governance. And the fact that the Labour Government, under Callaghan, had agreed to the imposition of an austerity program - along corporatist lines but against the interests of its traditional supporters - mandated by the International Monetary Fund in 1976 in return for loans to cover the chronic state of indebtedness, helped pave the way for the idea that, as Thatcher had it, "there is no alternative" to neo-liberal solutions. The Thatcher revolution was, in this way, prepared by the organization of a certain level of political consent particularly within the middle classes that bore her to electoral victory. Programmatically she held an electoral mandate to roll back union power. Taking on the professional associations that held a great deal of power in areas such as education, health care, the judiciary and municipal governance was quite another matter. On this her cabinet (and her supporters) were notoriously divided and it took several years of bruising confrontations within her own party and in the media to hammer home the neo-liberal line. There is, she famously later declared, "no such thing as society, only individuals and," she subsequently added, "their families." All forms of social solidarity were to be dissolved in favor of individualism, private property, personal responsibility and family values. The ideological assault along those lines that flowed from Thatcher's rhetoric was relentless and eventually broadly successful.[12] "Economics are the method," she said, "but the object is to change the soul." And change it she did, though in ways that were by no means free of political costs as well as contradictory impulses as we will later see.

In October of 1979, Paul Volcker, Chairman of the US Federal Reserve Bank, engineered a draconian shift in US monetary policy.[13] The long-standing commitment in the US to the principles of the New Deal, which meant broadly Keynesian fiscal and monetary policies with full employment as the key objective, was abandoned in favor of a policy designed to quell inflation no matter what the consequences might be for employment or, for that matter, for the economies of countries (such as Mexico and Brazil) that were highly dependent upon economic conditions and sensitive to interest rate shifts in the US. The real rate of interest, that had often been negative during the double-digit inflationary surge of the 1970s, was rendered positive by fiat of the Federal Reserve. The nominal rate of interest was raised overnight (the move came to be known as "the Saturday night special") to close to 20 percent, deliberately plunging the US, and much of the rest of the world, into recession and unemployment. This shift, it was argued, was the only way out of the grumbling crisis of stagflation that had characterized the US and much of the global economy throughout the 1970s.

The Volcker shock, as it has since come to be known, could not be

---

12. The story of Thatcher's path to neo-liberalism is outlined in D. Yergin and J. Stanislaw, *The Commanding Heights: The Battle Between Government and Market Place that is Remaking the Modern World* (New York: Simon and Schuster, 1999).

13. L. Panitch and S. Gindin, "Global Finance and American Empire," forthcoming in *Socialist Register*, 2005.

consolidated without parallel shifts in government policies in all other arenas. Ronald Reagan's victory over Carter proved crucial. Reagan's advisors were convinced that Volcker's "medicine" for a sick and stagnant economy was right on target. Volcker was supported in and reappointed to his position as Chair of the Federal Reserve. The Reagan Administration's task was to provide the requisite political backing through further deregulation, tax cuts, budget cuts and attacks upon trade union and professional power. Reagan faced down PAT-CO, the air traffic controllers' union, in a lengthy and bitter strike. This signaled an all out assault on the powers of organized labor at the very moment when the Volcker-inspired recession was generating high levels of unemployment (ten percent or more). But PATCO was more than an ordinary union: it was also a white collar union that had the character of a skilled professional association and which was, therefore, an icon of middle class rather than working class unionism. The effect on the condition of labor across the board was dramatic – perhaps best captured by the fact that the Federal minimum wage that stood on a par with the poverty level in 1980 had fallen to 30 percent below that level by 1990. Reagan's appointments to positions of power on issues like environmental regulation, occupational safety and health, took the campaign against big government to ever-higher levels. The deregulation of everything from airlines and telecommunications to finance opened up new zones of untrammeled market freedoms for powerful corporate interests. The market, depicted ideologically as the great means to foster competition and innovation, was in practice to be the great vehicle for the consolidation of monopoly corporate and multinational powers as the nexus of class rule. Tax cuts for the rich simultaneously began the momentous shift towards greater social inequality and the restoration of upper class power.

Thomas Edsall (a journalist who covered Washington affairs for many years) published a prescient account of the class forces behind all this in 1984:

> During the 1970s, business refined its ability to act as a class, submerging competitive instincts in favor of joint, cooperative action in the legislative arena. Rather than individual companies

seeking only special favors . . . the dominant theme in the political strategy of business became a shared interest in the defeat of bills such as consumer protection and labor law reform, and in the enactment of favorable tax, regulatory and antitrust legislation.[14]

In order to realize this goal, business needed a political class instrument and a popular base. They therefore actively sought to capture the Republican Party as their own instrument. The formation of powerful political action committees to procure, as the old adage had it, "the best government that money could buy" was an important step. The supposedly "progressive" campaign finance laws of 1974 in effect legalized the financial corruption of politics. Political action committees could thereafter assure the financial domination of both political parties by corporate, moneyed and professional association interests. Corporate PACs that numbered 89 in 1974 had burgeoned to 1,467 by 1982. While these were willing to fund powerful incumbents of both parties provided their interests were served, they also systematically leaned towards supporting right wing challengers. The $5000 limit on each PAC's contribution to any one individual, forced PACs from different corporations and industries to work together: and that meant building alliances based on class interest. The willingness of the Republican Party to become the representative of "its dominant class constituency" during this period contrasted with the "ideologically ambivalent" attitude of the Democrats which grew out of "the fact that its ties to various groups in society are diffuse, and none of these groups – women, blacks, labor, the elderly, hispanics, urban political organizations – stands clearly larger than the others." The dependency of Democrats, furthermore, on "big money" contributions rendered many of them highly vulnerable to direct influence from business interests.[15] Domestic manufacturing, mining, forestry and agribusiness interests took the lead in this aspect of the class war that then unfolded.

The Republican Party needed, however, a solid electoral base if it was to colonize power effectively. It was around this time that Republicans sought an alliance with the Christian right. Jerry Falwell

14. T. Edsall, *The New Politics of Inequality* (New York: Norton, 1984) p. 217.
15. Ibid., on PACs see pp. 129–38; p. 235.

founded the "moral majority" movement in 1978 as the political arm
of a right-wing and very conservative Christianity. It appealed to the
cultural nationalism of the white working classes and their besieged
sense of moral righteousness (besieged because this class lived under
conditions of chronic economic insecurity and felt excluded from
many of the benefits that were being distributed through affirmative
action and other state programs). This "moral majority" could be
mobilized through coded if not blatant racism, homophobia and anti-
feminism. Not for the first, nor, it is to be feared, for the last time in
history has a social group willingly voted against its material, economic
and class interests for cultural, nationalist and religious reasons. From
then on the unholy alliance between big business and conservative
Christians steadily consolidated, eventually eradicating all liberal elements (significant and influential in the 1960s) from the Republican
Party and turning it into the relatively homogeneous right wing
electoral force of present times.

Reagan's election began the long process of consolidating the
political shift necessary to support the earlier monetarist shift towards
neo-liberalism. His policies, Edsall noted at the time, centered on:

> an across the board drive to reduce the scope and content of federal
> regulation of industry, the environment, the workplace, health care,
> and the relationship between buyer and seller. The Reagan admin-
> istration's drive toward deregulation was accomplished through
> sharp budget cuts reducing enforcement capabilities; through the
> appointment of anti-regulatory, industry-oriented agency person-
> nel; and finally through the empowering of the Office of Manage-
> ment and Budget with unprecedented authority to delay major
> regulations, to force major revisions in regulatory proposals, and
> through prolonged cost-benefit analyses, to effectively kill a wide
> range of regulatory initiatives.[16]

There was, however, one other concomitant shift that also impelled
the movement towards neo-liberal solutions, but this time at the global
level, during the 1970s. The OPEC oil price hike that came with the

16. Ibid., p. 235.

oil embargo of 1973, placed vast amounts of financial power at the disposal of the oil producing states such as Saudi Arabia, Kuwait, and Abu Dhabi. We now know from British intelligence reports that the US was actively preparing to invade these countries in 1973 in order to restore the flow of oil and bring down oil prices. We also know that the Saudis agreed at that time, presumably under military pressure if not open threat from the US, to recycle all of their petrodollars through the New York investment banks.[17] The latter suddenly found themselves in command of massive funds for which they needed to find profitable outlets. The options within the US, given the depressed economic conditions and low rates of return in the mid-1970s, were not good. More profitable opportunities had to be sought out abroad. But this required open entry and reasonably secure conditions for US controlled finance to operate in and across foreign territories. The New York investment banks looked to the US imperial tradition both to prize open new investment opportunities and to protect their foreign operations.

The US imperial tradition had been long in the making and to great degree defined itself against the imperial traditions of Britain, France, Holland, and other European powers.[18] While the US had toyed with colonial conquest at the end of the nineteenth century it evolved a more open system of imperialism without colonies during the twentieth century. The paradigm case was worked out in Nicaragua in the 1920s and 1930s, when US marines were deployed to protect US interests but found themselves embroiled in a lengthy and difficult guerilla insurgency led by Sandino. The answer was to find a local strongman – in this case Somoza – and to provide economic and military assistance to him and his family and immediate allies so that they could repress or buy off opposition and accumulate considerable

17. L. Alvarez, "Britain says U.S. planned to seize oil in '73 crisis," *New York Times*, January 4, 2004, p. A6. On the Saudi agreement to recycle petro-dollars through the US see P. Gowan, *The Global Gamble: Washington's Faustian Bid for World Dominance* (London: Verso, 1999).
18. D. Harvey, *The New Imperialism* (Oxford: Oxford University Press, 2003); N. Smith, *American Empire, Roosevelt's Geographer and the Prelude to Globalization* (Berkeley: University of California Press, 2003).

wealth and power for themselves. In return they would always support and if necessary promote US interests both in the country and in the region (in this case Central America) as a whole. This was the model that was deployed after World War II during the phase of global decolonization imposed upon the European powers at US insistence. For example, the CIA engineered the coup that overthrew the democratically elected Mossadeq government in Iran in 1953 and installed the Shah of Iran who gave the oil contract to US companies (and did not return the assets to the British companies that Mossadeq had nationalized). The Shah also became one of the key guardians of US interests in the Middle Eastern oil region. In the postwar period, much of the non-communist world was opened up to US domination by tactics of this sort. But this often entailed an anti-democratic (and even more emphatically anti-populist and anti-socialist/communist) strategy on the part of the US. This had the paradoxical effect of putting the US more and more in alliance with repressive military dictatorships and authoritarian regimes in the developing world (most spectacularly, of course, throughout Latin America). US interests consequently became more rather than less vulnerable in the struggle against international communism. Backing ever more repressive regimes was always in danger of proving counter-productive. While the consent of ruling elites could be purchased easily enough, the necessity of coercion to counter populist or social democratic movements associated the US with a long history of largely covert violence against popular movements.

It was in this context, that the surplus funds being recycled through the New York investment banks were dispersed throughout the world. Hitherto, most of the US investment that flowed to the developing world during the postwar period was of the direct sort, mainly concerned with the exploitation of raw material resources (oil, minerals, agricultural products) or the cultivation of specific markets (telecommunications, etc.). The New York investment banks had always been active internationally but after 1973 they became even more so though in ways that were less focused on direct investment.[19] This

---

19. Panitch and Gindin, "Global Finance and American Empire", *op. cit.*

required the liberalization of international credit and financial markets and the US began actively to promote and support this strategy almost immediately after the Volcker shock. The investment banks initially focused on direct lending to foreign governments. Hungry for credit, developing countries were, in effect, lured into the debt/credit trap and the investment banks (backed by US imperial power) were in a position to demand more favorable rates of return than could be had domestically.[20] Since the loans were designated in US dollars, any modest let alone precipitous rise in US interest rates could easily push vulnerable countries into default. The New York investment banks would then be heavily exposed to losses. The first major test case of this came in the wake of the Volcker shock which drove Mexico into default in 1982–4. The Reagan administration, which had seriously thought of withdrawing support for the International Monetary Fund in its first year in office, found a way to put together the powers of the US Treasury and the International Monetary Fund to resolve the difficulty by rolling over the debt in return for structural reforms. This required, of course, that the IMF shift from a Keynesian to a monetarist theoretical frame of reference (and this was quickly accomplished making the IMF a global center of influence for the new Monetarist orthodoxy in economic theory). In return for debt re-scheduling, Mexico was required to implement institutional reforms, such as cuts in welfare expenditures, relaxed labor laws and privatization, a procedure that came to be known as "structural adjustment." Mexico was thereby partially pushed into a growing column of neo-liberal state apparatuses and from then on the IMF became a key tool in the promotion and in many instances forced imposition of neo-liberal policies throughout the world.[21]

What the Mexico case demonstrated was one key difference between liberalism and neo-liberalism: under the former lenders take the losses that arise from bad investment decisions while under the latter the borrowers are forced by state and international powers to take

20. The many debt crises of the 80s are covered extensively in Gowan, *The Global Gamble, op. cit.*
21. Ibid.

on board the cost of debt repayment no matter what the consequences for the livelihood and well-being of the local population. If this required the surrender of assets to foreign companies at fire-sale prices, then so be it. With these innovations in financial markets at the global level, the systemic form of neo-liberalism was essentially rendered complete. As Dumenil and Levy show, the effect was to permit the upper classes in the US in particular to pump very high rates of return out of the rest of the world.[22]

The restoration of class power in the US also rested upon a certain reconfiguration of how class power was itself constituted. The separation between ownership and management (or between money capital earning dividends and interest and production/manufacturing capital looking to gain profit of enterprise out of the organization of production) had at various times produced conflicts between financiers and producers within the capitalist classes. In Britain, for example, government policy had long catered primarily to the requirements of the financiers in the City of London often to the detriment of the manufacturing interest and in the 1960s conflicts in the US between financiers and manufacturers had often surfaced. During the 1970s much of this conflict disappeared. The large corporations became more and more financial in their orientation even when, as in the automobile sector, they were engaging in production. The interests of owners and managers were fused by paying the latter in stock options. Stock values rather than production became the guiding light of economic activity and, as later became apparent with the collapse of companies like Enron, the speculative temptations that resulted could become overwhelming. The general effect was that financial interests (the power of the accountants rather than the engineers) gained the upper hand within the ruling classes and the ruling elites. Neo-liberalism meant, in short, the financialization of everything and the relocation of the power center of capital accumulation to owners and their financial institutions at the expense of other factions of capital. For this reason, the support of financial institutions and the integrity of the financial

---

22. G. Duménil and D. Lévy, "The Economics of US Imperialism at the Turn of the 21st Century," Unpublished MS, 2004.

system became the central concern of the collectivity of neo-liberal states (such as the group known as the G7) that increasingly dominated global politics.

The neo-liberal state

The fundamental mission of the neo-liberal state is to create a "good business climate" and therefore to optimize conditions for capital accumulation no matter what the consequences for employment or social well-being. This contrasts with the social democratic state that is committed to full employment and the optimization of the well-being of all of its citizens subject to the condition of maintaining adequate and stable rates of capital accumulation.

The neo-liberal state looks to further the cause of and to facilitate and stimulate (by tax breaks and other concessions as well as infrastructural provision at state expense if necessary) all business interests, arguing that this will foster growth and innovation and that this is the only way to eradicate poverty and to deliver, in the long run, higher living standards to the mass of the population. The neo-liberal state is particularly assiduous in seeking the privatization of assets as a means to open up fresh fields for capital accumulation. Sectors formerly run or regulated by the state (transportation, telecommunications, oil and other natural resources, utilities, social housing, education) are turned over to the private sphere or deregulated. The free mobility of capital between sectors and regions is regarded as crucial to reviving profit rates and all barriers to that free movement (such as planning controls) have to be removed except in those areas crucial to "the national interest" (however that may be conveniently defined). The watchword of the neo-liberal state is, therefore, "flexibility" (in labor markets and in the deployment of investment capital). It trumpets the virtues of competition while actually opening the market to centralized capital and monopoly power.

Internally, the neo-liberal state is hostile to (and in some instances overtly repressive of) all forms of social solidarity (such as the trade unions or other social movements that acquired considerable power in the social democratic state) that put restraints on capital accumulation. It withdraws from welfare provision and diminishes its role as far as possible in the arenas of health care, public education and social services that had been so central to the operations of the social democratic state. The social safety net is reduced to a bare minimum. This does not mean the elimination of all forms of regulatory activity or government intervention. Bureaucratic rules to ensure "accountability" and the "cost effectiveness" of public sectors that cannot be privatized flourish (Margaret Thatcher, for example, sought and achieved strong regulatory control over universities in Britain). Public-private partnerships are favored in which the public sector bears all of the risk and the corporate sector reaps all of the profit. Business interests get to write legislation and to determine public policies in such a way as to advantage themselves. If necessary the state will resort to coercive legislation and policing tactics (anti-picketing rules, for example) to disperse or repress collective forms of opposition. Forms of surveillance and policing multiply (in the US incarceration became a key state strategy to deal with problems arising among discarded workers and marginalized populations).

Externally, neo-liberal states seek the reduction of barriers to movement of capital across borders and the opening of markets (for both commodities and money capital) to global forces of capital accumulation, sometimes competitive but more often monopolistic (though always with the opt-out provision to refuse anything "against the national interest"). The powers of international competition and the ideology of globalization are used to discipline internal opposition at the same time as new terrains for highly profitable and in some instances even neo-colonial capitalistic activity are opened up abroad. In this sphere too, large corporate capitalist interests typically collaborate with government power in policy making as well as in the creation of new international institutional arrangements (such as the WTO or the IMF and the Bank of International Settlements).

The neo-liberal state is particularly solicitous of financial institutions. It seeks not only to facilitate their spreading influence but also to guarantee the integrity and solvency of the financial system at no matter what cost. State power is used to bail out or avert financial failures (such as the US savings and loans crisis of 1987–8 and the three trillion dollar collapse of the hedge fund Long Term Capital Management in 1997–8). Internationally it operates through institutions such as the IMF to shelter investment banks from the threat of default on debts and in effect covers, to the best of its ability, exposures of financial interests to risk and uncertainty in international markets. This connectivity of the neo-liberal state to the protection of financial interests both promotes and reflects the consolidation of bourgeois class power around processes of financialization. In the event of a conflict between the integrity of the financial system and the well-being of a population, the neo-liberal state will choose the former.

The neo-liberal state is profoundly anti-democratic, even as it frequently seeks to disguise this fact. Governance by elites is favored and a strong preference for government by executive order and by judicial decision arises at the expense of the former centrality of democratic and parliamentary decision-making. What remains of representative democracy is overwhelmed if not, as in the US, totally though legally corrupted by money power. Strong institutions are created, such as central banks (like the Federal Reserve in the US) and quasi-governmental institutions internally and the IMF and the WTO on the international stage, that are entirely outside of democratic influence, auditing, accountability and control. In the neo-liberal view, mass democracy is equated with "mob rule" and this typically produces all of the barriers to capital accumulation that so threatened the power of the upper classes in the 1970s. The preferred form of governance is that of the "public–private partnership" in which state and key business interests collaborate closely together to coordinate their activities around the aim of enhancing capital accumulation. The result is that the regulated get to write the rules of regulation while "public" decision-making becomes ever more opaque.

The neo-liberal state emphasizes the importance of personal and individual freedom, liberty and responsibility, particularly in the market place. Social success or failure is therefore interpreted in terms of personal entrepreneurial virtues or failings rather than attributable to any systemic properties (such as the class exclusions typical of capitalism). Opposition within the rules of the neo-liberal state is typically confined to questions of individual human rights and "rights discourses" of all kinds have, as a result, blossomed since 1980 or so as a primary site of "radical" and oppositional politics. Solutions and remedies to problems have to be sought by individuals (and, recall, corporations are legally defined as individuals) through the courts. Since access to the latter is nominally egalitarian but in practice extremely expensive (be it an individual suing over negligent practices or a country suing the US for violation of WTO rules – a procedure that can cost up to a million dollars which is equivalent to the annual budget of some small impoverished countries) the outcomes are strongly biased towards those with money power. Class bias in decision making within the judiciary is, in any case, pervasive if not assured. It should not be surprising that the primary collective means of action under neo-liberalism are then defined and articulated through non-elected (and in many instances elite-led) advocacy groups for various kinds of rights. NGOs have grown and proliferated under neo-liberalism, giving rise to the illusion that opposition mobilized outside of the state apparatus and within some separate entity called "civil society" is the powerhouse of oppositional politics and social transformation.

By this account we clearly see that neo-liberalism has not made the state or particular institutions of the state (such as the courts) irrelevant, as many commentators on both the right and the left have argued in recent years. There has, however, been a radical reconfiguration of state institutions and practices (particularly with respect to the balance between coercion and consent, the balance between the powers of capital and of popular movements, and the balance between executive and judicial power on the one hand and parliamentary democratic power on the other).

The neo-liberal state internalizes some fundamental structural contradictions. Authoritarianism (embedded in dominant class relations whose reproduction is fundamental to the social order) sits uneasily with ideals of individual freedoms. While it may be crucial to preserve the integrity of the financial system the irresponsible and self-aggrandizing individualism of operators within the financial system produce speculative volatility and chronic instability. While the virtues of competition are placed up front the reality is the increasing consolidation of monopoly power within a few centralized multinational corporations. At the popular level, the drive towards freedom of the individual person can all too easily run amok and produce social incoherence. The need to perpetuate dominant power relations necessarily creates, therefore, relations of oppression that thwart the drive towards individualized freedom. In the international arena the competitive volatility of neo-liberalism threatens the stability and status of hegemonic power. A hegemonic power, such as the US, may then be provoked into repressive measures and actions designed to protect the asymmetries of economic relations that preserve its hegemony. To all of these contradictions we must then add the potentiality for a burgeoning disparity between the declared public aims of neo-liberalism – the well-being of all – and its actual consequences – the restoration of class power.

We will take up these contradictory elements later. But, clearly, neo-liberalism is an unstable and evolving regime of accumulation rather than a fixed and harmoniously functional configuration of political economic power. This paves the way for looking at neo-conservatism as a potential response to its inherent contradictions.

Implantations, diffusions and evolutions

Consider, then, the ways in which neo-liberal politics and policies actually became embedded within the historical geography of global capitalism after the mid-1970s. Clearly, the UK and the US led the way. But in neither Britain nor the US was the turn unproblematic. In Britain neo-liberal political reforms were fought over during a long decade of class confrontation and struggle, with the prolonged and bitter miners' strike of 1984–5 a central motif. While Thatcher could successfully privatize social housing and the public utilities, core public services such as the national health care system and public education proved immune to anything other than tinkering at the edges. And since many in her own party were initially unconvinced of the direction she had chosen, all sorts of barriers were thrown up to the realization of her objectives. Her re-election in 1983 owed far more to the rising tide of nationalism she cultivated around the Falklands/Malvinas war than to any real successes down the neo-liberal road. In the US the transformation during the Reagan years was less conflictual and of stronger import. The "Keynesian compromise" of the 1960s had never got close to the achievements of social democratic states in Europe and the opposition to neo-liberalism was less combative. Reagan was also heavily preoccupied with the Cold War and launched an arms race that entailed a certain kind of deficit-funded military Keynesianism of specific benefit to his electoral majority in the South and West. The rising Federal deficits provided a convenient excuse to gut social programs.[23]

In spite of all the rhetoric about curing sick economies, neither Britain nor the US achieved high levels of economic performance in the 1980s, suggesting that neo-liberalism might well not be the answer to the capitalists' prayers. To be sure, inflation was brought down and interest rates could fall, but this was all purchased at the expense of high rates of unemployment (averaging 7.5 percent during the Reagan years, for example). On the other hand, the collapse of the French socialist/communist attempt to deepen state control (by nationalization of banks) and to foster growth through conquest of the internal market meant the erasure of any left alternative after the mid-1980s. So where was an adequate alternative?

The 1980s in fact belonged to Japan, the East Asian "tiger" economies and West Germany as powerhouses of the global economy. The fact that these proved very successful in spite of radically different institutional arrangements makes it difficult to argue for some simple turn to (let alone imposition of) neo-liberalism on the world stage as an obvious economic palliative. To be sure, in both Japan and West Germany, the central banks generally followed a monetarist line (the West German Bundesbank was particularly assiduous in combating inflation). But in West Germany the unions remained very strong and wage levels relatively high. One of the effects was to stimulate a high rate of technological innovation and this kept West Germany well

23. D. Stockman, *The Triumph of Politics: Why the Reagan Revolution Failed* (New York: Harper-Collins, 1986).

ahead of the field in international competition. Export-led growth could power the country forward as a global leader. In Japan, independent unions were weak or non-existent, but state investment in technological and organizational change and the tight relationship between corporations and financial institutions (an arrangement that also proved felicitous in West Germany) generated an astonishing export-led growth performance, very much at the expense of other capitalist economies such as the UK and the US.[24] Such growth as there was in the 1980s (and the aggregate rate of growth in the world was lower even than that of the troubled 1970s) did not depend, therefore, on neo-liberalism. By the end of the decade those countries which had taken the stronger neo-liberal path still seemed to be in economic difficulty. It was hard not to conclude that the West German and Japanese "regimes" of accumulation were deserving of emulation. Many European states therefore resisted neo-liberal reforms and increasingly found ways to preserve much of their social democratic heritage while moving, in some cases fairly successfully, towards the West German model.[25] In Asia, the Japanese model implanted under authoritarian systems of governance (one of the hidden features of neo-liberalism more generally) in South Korea, Taiwan and Singapore also proved viable and consistent with reasonable equality of distribution. But in one respect the West German and the Japanese models were not successful: and this was from the standpoint of the restoration of class power. The rapid increases in social inequality to be found in the UK and particularly in the US during the 1980s were held in check elsewhere. If the project was to restore class power to the top elites, then neo-liberalism was clearly the answer. The question therefore arose of how to accomplish this on the world stage when neo-liberalism was failing to stimulate real growth.

In this regard the accounts of Dumenil and Levy supplemented by those of Brenner, Gowan and Pollin provide much of the necessary

---

24. C. Johnson, *MITI and the Japanese Miracle* (Stanford: Stanford University Press, 1982).
25. Much of this was explored in the 1980s with the aid of "regulation theory" – see R. Boyer, *La Théorie de la Régulation: Une Analyse Critique* (Paris: La Découverte, 1986).

evidence.[26] From these I distill three distinctive components. First, the turn to financialization that had begun in the 1970s accelerated during the 1990s. Foreign direct investment and portfolio investment rose rapidly throughout the capitalist world. Financial markets experienced a powerful wave of innovation and became far more important instruments of coordination. This undermined the close tie of exclusivity between corporations and the banks that had served the West Germans and the Japanese so well during the 1980s. The Japanese economy went into a tail spin (led by a collapse in land and property markets) and the banking sector was found to be in a parlous state. The hasty re-unification of Germany created stresses and the technological advantage that the Germans had earlier commanded dissipated, making it necessary to challenge more deeply the social democratic tradition there. German resistance remained strong and as late as 2004, residual battles were still being fought over attempts to eliminate the social democratic achievements in realms such as state pensions and free higher education. Secondly, the Wall Street/IMF/Treasury complex that came to dominate economic policy in the Clinton years was not only able to persuade, cajole and (thanks to structural adjustment programs) to coerce developing countries into a neo-liberal path. The US also used the carrot of preferential access to the huge US consumer market to persuade many countries to reform their economies along neo-liberal lines, most particularly in opening their capital markets to the penetration of US finance capital. These policies produced a rapid economic expansion in the US in the 1990s. The US looked as if it had the answer and that its policies were worthy of emulation, even if the full employment achieved entailed employment at relatively low rates of pay (the mass of the population actually experienced very little improvement if not a net loss in well-being during these years as Pollin shows[27]). Flexibility in labor markets began to pay off for the US and put competitive pressures on the more rigid systems that prevailed in

---

26. G. Duménil and D. Lévy, *Economie Marxiste du Capitalisme* (Paris: La Découverte, 2003); R. Brenner, *The Boom and the Bubble: The US in the World Economy* (London: Verso, 2002); Gowan, *The Global Gamble, op. cit.*; R. Pollin, *Contours of Descent* (London: Verso, 2003).

27. Pollin, Contours of Descent *op. cit.*

Europe and Japan. The real secret of US success, however, was that it was now able to pump high rates of return into the country from its operations (both direct and portfolio investments) in the rest of the world. It was this flow of tribute from the rest of the world that founded much of the affluence achieved in the 1990s. Thirdly, the global diffusion of the new monetarist economic orthodoxy also exerted a powerful ideological role. As early as 1982, Keynesian economics had been eradicated from the corridors of the IMF and the World Bank and by the end of the decade most economics departments in the US research universities – and these helped train most of the world's economists – had fallen in line with broadly monetarist arguments.

All of these strands came together in the fierce ideological offensive that produced the so-called "Washington Consensus" of the mid 1990s.[28] The effect was to define the US and UK models of neo-liberalism as the answer to global problems and thereby put considerable pressure even on Japan and Europe (to say nothing of the rest of the world) to take the neo-liberal road. Ironically, it was Clinton and then Blair who, from the center-left, did the most to consolidate the role of neo-liberalism both at home and internationally. The formation of the WTO was the high point of institutional reform on the world stage. Programmatically, the WTO set neo-liberal standards and rules for interaction in the global economy. Its primary objective, however, was to open up as much of the world as possible to unhindered capital flow (though always with the caveat clause of protection of key "national interests"), for this was the foundation of the capacity of the US financial power as well as that of Europe and Japan, to exact tribute from the rest of the world.

This narrative sketch of the uneven geographical development of neo-liberalism suggests that its implantation was as much an outcome of diversification, innovation and competition (sometimes of the monopolistic sort) between national, regional and in some instances even metropolitan models of governance and economic development,

28. B. Fine (ed.) *Development Policy in the Twenty-First Century: Beyond the Post-Washington Consensus* (London: Routledge, 2001).

rather than the imposition of some model orthodoxy by some
hegemonic power, such as the US. That this was the case can best
be illustrated by a brief examination of the strange case of China.

The strange case of China

In December 1978, faced with the dual difficulties of political uncertainty in the wake of Mao's death in 1976 and several years of
economic stagnation, the Chinese leadership under Deng Xiaoping
announced a program of economic reform. This coincided – and it is
very hard to consider it as anything other than a conjunctural accident
of world-historical significance – with the turn to neo-liberal solutions
in Britain and the United States. The outcome has been a particular
kind of neo-liberalism interdigitated with authoritarian centralized
control. But for much of East and SouthEast Asia – in South Korea,
Taiwan and Singapore most noticeably – this connection between
dictatorial rule and neo-liberal economics had already been well-
established. As the formative case of Chile had early on demonstrated,
dictatorship and neo-liberalism were in no way incompatible with each
other.

While egalitarianism as a long-term goal for China was not abandoned, Deng argued that individual and local initiative had to be
unleashed in order to increase productivity and spark economic
growth. The corollary, that certain levels of inequality would inevitably arise, was well understood as something that would need to be
tolerated. Under the slogan of xiaokang – the concept of an ideal
society that provides well for all its citizens – Deng focussed on "four
modernizations" (in agriculture, industry, education, and science and
defense). The reforms strove to bring market forces to bear internally
within the Chinese economy. The idea was to stimulate competition
between state-owned firms and thereby spark, it was hoped, innovation and growth. Market pricing was introduced but this was probably
far less significant than the rapid devolution of political-economic
power to the regions and to the localities. To supplement this effort,
China was also to be opened up, albeit in a very limited way and under

strict State supervision, to foreign trade and foreign investment, thus ending China's isolation from the world market. One aim of this opening to the outside was to procure technology transfers. The other was to gain enough foreign reserves to buy in the necessary means to support a stronger internal dynamic of economic growth.[29]

China's extraordinary subsequent economic evolution would not have taken the path and registered the achievements it did, had not the turn towards neo-liberal policies on the world stage opened up a space for China's tumultuous entry and incorporation into the world market. China's emergence as a global economic power must in part be considered, therefore, as an unintended consequence of the neo-liberal turn in the advanced capitalist world.

To put it this way in no way diminishes the significance of the tortuous path of the internal reform movement within China itself. For what the Chinese had to learn, among many other things, was that the market can do very little to transform an economy without a parallel shift in class relations, private property and all the other institutional arrangements that typically found a thriving capitalist economy. The evolution along this path was both slow and frequently marked by tensions and crises. It became clear during the

29. It is hard to keep up with the pace of change in China. Reports from the Asian Development Bank, the Asian Monitor coupled with reports in the financial press allow some rough assessments to be made. Si-ming Li and Wing-shing Tang, *China's Regions, Polity, and Economy: A Study of Spatial Transformation in the Post-Reform Era* (Hong Kong: The Chinese University Press, 2000); D. Hale and L. Hale, "China Takes Off," *Foreign Affairs*, 82 No.6 (2003) pp. 36–53. See H. McRae, "Working for the Yangtze dollar," *The Independent Review*, November 18, 2003, pp. 2–3; K. Bradsher, "Is China the next bubble?" *New York Times*, January 18, 2004, Section 3, 1 and 9; T. Crampton, "Asia's rally defies most expectations," *International Herald Tribune*, January 21, p. 17; L. Uchitelle, "When the Chinese consumer is king," *New York Times*, December 14, 2003, Week in Review, p. 5; K. Bradsher, "Consumerism grows in China, with Beijing's blessing," *New York Times*, December 1, 2003, C15; K. Bradsher, "China's Strange Hybrid Economy," *New York Times*, November 21, 2003, C5; J. Kahn, "China seen ready to conciliate U.S. on trade and jobs," *New York Times*, September 2, 2003, A1 and C2; K. Bradsher, "Like Japan in the 1980's, China Poses Big Economic challenge," *New York Times*, March 2, 2004, A1 and C2; T. Fishman, "The Chinese Century," *New York Times Magazine*, July 4, 2004, pp. 24–51.

1980s, for example, that most of China's phenomenal growth rate was being powered outside of the centralized state sector rather than, as the Chinese had hoped, through a bureaucratically organized state sector rendered more productive and competitive by the market reforms and a more flexible approach to market pricing mechanisms. This was true even though the State Owned Enterprises were much favored (partly through regulatory and political controls but also by differential access to state regulated credit) over the numerous local township and village enterprises that arose out of local initiatives as well as over indigenous private capital. But if the dynamo of growth lay in the local or private rather than in the central state sector, then sustaining growth demanded and eventually required further decentralization and privatization. The parallel political demand for liberalization that culminated in the spectacular repression of the student movement in Tiananmen Square in 1989 signaled a tremendous tension in the political realm that paralleled the economic pressure towards further liberalization.

The response to the events of 1989 was to initiate yet another wave of economic reforms, several of which moved China closer to neo-liberal orthodoxy. Wang summarizes these as follows:

> monetary policy became a prime means of control; there was a significant readjustment in the foreign currency exchange rate, moving towards a unified rate; exports and foreign trade came to be managed by mechanisms of competition and assumption of responsibility for profits or losses; the 'dual track' pricing system was reduced in scope; the Shanghai Pudong development zone was fully opened and the various regional development zones were all put on track.[30]

The first wave of foreign direct investment into China met, however, with very mixed results. It was initially channeled into four special economic zones in southern coastal regions (where

---

30. Wang Hui, edited by T. Huters, *China's New Order: Society, Politics and Economy in Transition* (Cambridge, Mass.: Harvard University Press, 2003) p. 66.

proximity to Hong Kong was deemed to be helpful). These zones "had the initial objective of producing goods for export to earn foreign exchange. They also acted as social and economic laboratories where foreign technologies and managerial skills could be observed. They offered a range of inducements to foreign investors, including tax holidays, early remittances of profits and better infrastructure facilities." Subsequently the Chinese government designated several "open coastal cities" as well as "open economic regions" for foreign investment of any type. But initial attempts by foreign firms to colonize the internal China market in areas like automobiles and manufactured goods did not fare at all well. Ford's joint venture barely survived and General Motors failed in the early 1990s. The only sectors where clear successes were recorded in the early years were in those industries oriented to exports of goods with high labor content. More than two thirds of the foreign direct investment that came in during the early 1990s (and an even greater percentage that survived) was organized by the overseas Chinese (particularly operating out of Hong Kong but also from Taiwan). The weak legal protections for capitalist enterprises put a premium on informal local relations and trust networks that the overseas Chinese were in a privileged position to exploit.[31]

The massive bankruptcies of the village and township enterprises in the manufacturing sector in 1997–8, spilling over into many of the state-owned enterprises in the main urban centers, proved a turning point. Pricing mechanisms and competition then took over from the devolution of power from the central state to regions, export zones and localities as the core process impelling the restructuring of the economy. The effect was to severely damage if not destroy much of the state-organized sector and create a vast wave of unemployment. Reports of considerable labor unrest abounded and the Chinese Government was faced with the problem of absorbing vast labor

31. Yasheng Huang, *Foreign Direct Investment in China: An Asian Perspective* (New York: Columbia University Press, 1998); Si-ming Li and Wing-shing Tang, *China's Regions, Polity, and Economy, op. cit.*; J. Kahn, "Made in China, Bought in China: Multinationals Succeed, Two Decades Later," *New York Times*, January 5, 2003, Section 3, 1 and 10.

surpluses if it was to survive.[32] Since 1998, the Chinese have sought to confront this problem through debt-financed investments in huge mega-projects to transform physical infrastructures. They are proposing a far more ambitious project (costing at least $60 billion) than the already huge Three Gorges Dam to divert water from the Yangtze to the Yellow River. Astonishing rates of urbanization (no less than 42 cities have expanded beyond the one million population mark since 1992) have entailed huge investments of fixed capital. New subway systems and highways are being built in major cities, 8,500 miles of new railroads are proposed to integrate the interior to the economically dynamic coastal zone, including a high-speed link between Shanghai and Beijing and a link into Tibet. The Olympic Games is prompting heavy investment (as well as massive population displacement) in Beijing. This effort is far larger *in toto* than that which the United States undertook during the 1950s and 1960s in constructing the interstate highway system and has the potential to absorb surpluses of capital for several years to come. It is, however, deficit financed (in classic Keynesian style) and that entails high risks since if the investments do not return their value to the accumulation process in due course, then a fiscal crisis of the state will quickly engulf China with serious consequences for economic development and social stability.[33]

But the crisis of 1997–8 also opened the way for private (particularly foreign) capital to take over bankrupt state enterprises without taking on any of their social obligations (such as pension and welfare rights). The door now became wide open for foreign capital, particularly from the

32. J. Khan, "China's Leaders Manage Class Conflict Carefully," *New York Times*, January 25, Week in Review, p. 5; E. Eckholm, "Where Workers, Too, Rust, Bitterness Boils Over," *New York Times*, March 20, 2002, A4; E. Eckholm, "A Ming Town's Sullen Peace Masks the Bitter Legacy of China's Labor Strategy," *New York Times*, April 14, 2002, International Section, 8; E. Rosenthal, "Workers' Plight Brings New Militancy in China," *New York Times*, March 10, 2003, International Section A8; J. Kahn, "Beijing Leaders Populist Touch Is Not Felt by Most Rural Poor," *New York Times*, January 10, 2004, A5.

33. J. Kahn, "China Gambles on Big Projects for its Stability," *New York Times*, Jan 13, 2003, A1 and A8; H. French, "New Boomtowns Change Path of China's Growth," *New York Times*, July 26, 2004, A1 and A8.

rest of East and South East Asia but also from the US and Europe, to restructure much of the Chinese manufacturing sector at will under conditions of massive labor surpluses (nearly 50 million workers laid off from the state sector during the 1990s and a growing mass of 150 million unemployed rural workers to draw upon) and easy state-backed credit. By 2002, over 40 percent of China's GDP was accounted for by foreign direct investment. China had by then become the largest recipient of foreign direct investment in the developing world (and was widely expected to assume second place in the world for FDI after the US as early as 2004).[34] Multinationals interested in the China market were now in a position to exploit it profitably. General Motors, for example, that had lost on its failed venture in the early 1990s re-entered the market at the end of the decade and was reporting far higher profits on its Chinese venture by 2003 compared with its domestic US operations.[35] Foreign investors, though still technically at a disadvantage in relation to by then uncompetitive state enterprises, were, according to many reports, actually advantaged relative to the indigenous private sector that still suffered from significant exclusions and the hidden costs of corruption within the state and state-dominated banking apparatus. This contributed to the dominant role of foreign (including overseas Chinese) investment in manufacturing relative to indigenous capital.

But the legal institutional basis of this giant movement remained uncertain. Informal land and property markets had arisen particularly in peripheral urban areas. This was accompanied by powerful waves of primitive accumulation. Commune leaders, for example, frequently assumed de facto property rights to communal land and assets in negotiations with foreign investors and these rights were later confirmed as belonging to them as individuals, in effect enclosing the commons to the benefit of the few and to the detriment of the mass of the population. In the confusion of transition, writes Wang, "a

---

34. Congressional-Executive Commission on China, Statement of Yasheng Huang, "Is China Playing by the Rules? Free Trade, Fair Trade, and WTO Compliance," September 24, 2003, http://www.cecc.gov/pages/hearings/092403/huang.php

35. K. Bradsher, "GM to Speed Up Expansion in China," *New York Times*, June 8, 2004, W1 and 8.

significant amount of national property 'legally' and illegally was transferred to the personal economic advantage of a small minority."[36] Speculation in land and property markets, particularly in urban areas, became rife even in the absence of clear systems of property rights. In 2004, however, the rights of private property were formally enshrined in the Chinese constitution, signaling a move towards the confirmation of informal institutional arrangements for indigenous entrepreneurs more typical of a capitalist social order. The admission of business entrepreneurs into the communist party set up the possibility for the emergence of some kind of "public-private" governance system that, as we have shown, is characteristic of neo-liberal states.

China has, in short, been experiencing a radical process of bourgeois and capitalist-class formation (rather than a restoration of pre-existing class power as in the US).[37] Communism had never eradicated structural inequalities in the Chinese economy of course. The differentiation between town and country was even written into law. But under conditions of reform, writes Wang, "this structural inequality quickly transformed itself into disparities in income among different classes, social strata, and regions, leading rapidly to social polarization."[38] China has also evolved (rather as happened in the Reagan era in the U.S.) a very distinctive (and almost certainly unstable) mix of Keynesian deficit-financing of infrastructural projects under state direction and a more free-wheeling neo-liberalism of privatization and consolidation of class power under authoritarian rule. The pressures and opportunities that came with China opening up to foreign trade, capital inflows and foreign influences undoubtedly played a critical role. And China's accession to the World Trade Organization in 2001 in principal binds it, after a period of transition, to abide by neo-liberal rules on the world market. But the power of the state and of the communist party (and their ability to engage with authoritarian practices at will) as well as the peculiar conditions of the transition process make for some very distinctive features to the Chinese case. It

36. Wang Hui, *China's New Order*, op. cit., p. 53.
37. M. Hart-Landsberg and P. Burkett, "China and Socialism: Market Reforms and Class Struggle," *Monthly Review*, 56, No.3.
38. Wang Hui, *China's New Order*, op. cit., pp. 57–8.

remains to be seen if the Chinese configuration will in turn exercise strong influences on the general path of capitalist development by its sheer competitive power on the world stage. The explicit authoritarianism of the Chinese instance is particularly troubling in view of the more covert anti-democratic tendencies implicit in neo-liberalism. It suggests that the turn towards neo-conservatism, not only in the US but also in some European countries (Italy stands out), may be a deepening of the anti-democratic tendencies within neo-liberalism rather than a radical departure. And China's competitive weight may add momentum to this trend towards authoritarianism.

However, China is not alone as a potential competitor on the global stage, for the class transformations occurring in Russia and India, just to cite two other examples, may also exert influences well beyond their borders.[39] And a new systems alliance, such as that which formed between Brazil, India, China, South Africa and others at the Cancun conference could well signal the emergence of a completely different power force in global politics just as important, if not potentially more so, than the alliance that came together at Bandung in 1955 to create a bloc of non-aligned countries in the midst of Cold War polarization. All of this shows, however, that we are not confronting any simple "export" of neo-liberalism from some hegemonic center. The development of neo-liberalism must be regarded as a decentered and unstable evolutionary process characterized by uneven geographical developments and strong competitive pressures between a variety of dynamic centers of political-economic power.

Achievements: the resurgence of accumulation by dispossession

In what ways can it be said that the neo-liberal turn has resolved the problems of flagging capital accumulation? Its actual record in stimu-

39. Yasheng Huang and Tarun Khanna, "Can India Overtake China?" *China Now*, April 3, 2004, http://www.chinanowmag.com/business/business.htm. See also Yergin and Stanislaw, *The Commanding Heights, op.cit.* chapters 8 and 10.

lating economic growth is nothing short of dismal. Aggregate growth rates stood at 3.5 percent or so in the 1960s and even during the troubled 1970s fell only to 2.4 percent. But the subsequent global growth rates of 1.4 percent and 1.1 percent for the 1980s and 1990s (and a rate that barely touches 1 percent since 2000) indicate that neo-liberalism has broadly failed to stimulate world-wide growth.[40] Why, then, are so many persuaded that neo-liberalism is the "only alter-native" and that it has been so successful? Two reasons stand out. First, the volatility of uneven geographical development has accelerated permitting certain territories to advance spectacularly (at least for a time) at the expense of others. If, for example, the 1980s belonged largely to Japan, the Asian "tigers" and West Germany, and if the 1990s belonged to the US and the UK, then the fact that "success" was to be had somewhere obscured the fact that neo-liberalism was generally failing. Secondly, neo-liberalism has been a huge success from the standpoint of the upper classes. It has either restored class power to ruling elites (as in the US and to some extent in Britain) or created conditions for capitalist class formation (as in China, India, Russia, and elsewhere). In both instances it is the increase in inequality that has counted.[41] With the media dominated by upper class interests, the myth could be propagated that territories failed because they were not competitive enough (thereby setting the stage for even more neo-liberal reforms). Increased social inequality within a territory was necessary to encourage the entrepreneurial risk and innovation that conferred competitive power and stimulated growth. If conditions among the lower classes deteriorated, this was because they failed, usually for personal and cultural reasons, to enhance their own human capital (through dedication to education, the acquisition of a protestant work ethic, submission to work discipline and flexibility, and the like).

40. World Commission on the Social Dimension of Globalization, *A Fair Globalization: Creating Opportunities for All* (Geneva: International Labor Office, 2004).

41. The trend to increasing social inequality in the US in comparative perspec-tive is examined in "Task Force on Inequality and American Democracy", *American Democracy, op.cit.* The technical reports also contain pertinent comparative information.

Particular problems arose, in short, because of lack of competitive strength or because of personal, cultural and political failings. In a Darwinian world, the argument went, only the fittest should and do survive. Systemic problems were masked under a blizzard of ideological pronouncements and under a plethora of localized crises.

If the main achievements of neo-liberalism have been redistributive rather than generative, then ways had to be found to transfer assets and redistribute wealth and income either from the mass of the population towards the upper classes or from vulnerable to richer countries. I have elsewhere provided an account of these mechanisms under the rubric of "accumulation by dispossession."[42] By this I mean the continuation and proliferation of accumulation practices that Marx had treated as "primitive" or "original" during the rise of capitalism. These include the commodification and privatization of land and the forceful expulsion of peasant populations (as in Mexico and India in recent times); conversion of various forms of property rights (common, collective, state, etc.) into exclusive private property rights; suppression of rights to the commons; commodification of labor power and the suppression of alternative (indigenous) forms of production and consumption; colonial, neo-colonial and imperial processes of appropriation of assets (including natural resources); monetization of exchange and taxation, particularly of land; the slave trade (which continues particularly in the sex industry); and usury, the national debt and, most devastating of all, the use of the credit system as radical means of primitive accumulation. The state, with its monopoly of violence and definitions of legality, plays a crucial role in both backing and promoting these processes. To this list of mechanisms we may now add a raft of additional techniques, such as the extraction of rents from patents and intellectual property rights and the diminution or erasure of various forms of common property rights (such as state pensions, paid vacations, access to education and health care) won through a generation or more of social democratic class struggle. The proposal to privatize all state pension rights (pioneered in Chile under the dictatorship) is, for example, one of the cherished objectives of the neo-liberals in the US.

42. Harvey, *The New Imperialism, op. cit.*, chapter 4.

While in the cases of China and Russia, it might be reasonable to refer to recent events in "primitive" and "original" terms, the practices that restored class power to capitalist elites in the US and elsewhere are best described as an on-going process of accumulation by dispossession that rose rapidly to prominence under neo-liberalism. I isolate four main elements:

1. Privatization

The corporatization, commodification and privatization of hitherto public assets has been a signal feature of the neo-liberal project. Its primary aim has been to open up new fields for capital accumulation in domains hitherto regarded off-limits to the calculus of profitability. Public utilities of all kinds (water, telecommunications, transportation), social welfare provision (social housing, education, health care, pensions), public institutions (such as universities, research laboratories, prisons) and even warfare (as illustrated by the "army" of private contractors operating alongside the armed forces in Iraq) have all been privatized to some degree throughout the capitalist world. The intellectual property rights established through the so-called TRIPS agreement within the WTO defines genetic materials, seed plasmas, and all manner of other products, as private property. Rents for use can then be extracted from populations whose practices had played a crucial role in the development of these genetic materials. Biopiracy is rampant and the pillaging of the world's stockpile of genetic resources is well under way to the benefit of a few large pharmaceutical companies. The escalating depletion of the global environmental commons (land, air, water) and proliferating habitat degradations that preclude anything but capital intensive modes of agricultural production have likewise resulted from the wholesale commodification of nature in all its forms. The commodification (through tourism) of cultural forms, histories and intellectual creativity entails wholesale dispossessions (the music industry is notorious for the appropriation and exploitation of grassroots culture and creativity). As in the past, the power of the state is frequently used to force such processes through even against popular will. The rolling back of regulatory frameworks designed to protect labor and the environment from degradation has entailed the loss of rights. The reversion of common property rights won through years of hard class struggle (the right to a state pension, to welfare, to national health care) into the private domain has been one of the most egregious of all policies of dispossession pursued in the name of neo-liberal orthodoxy. All of these processes amount to the transfer of assets from the public and popular realms to the private and class-privileged domains. Privatization, Arundhati Roy argues with respect to the Indian case, entails "the transfer of productive public assets from the state to private companies. Productive assets include natural resources. Earth, forest, water, air. These are the assets that the state holds in trust for the people it represents . . . To snatch these away and sell them as stock to private companies is a process of barbaric dispossession on a scale that has no parallel in history."[43]

2. Financialization

The strong wave of financialization that set in after 1980 has been marked by its speculative and predatory style. The total daily turnover of financial transactions in international markets which stood at $2.3 billion in 1983 had risen to $130 billion by 2001. This $40 trillion annual turnover in 2001 compares to the estimated $800 billion that would be required to support international trade and productive investment flows.[44] Deregulation allowed the financial system to become one of the main centers of redistributive activity through speculation, predation, fraud and thievery. Stock promotions, ponzi schemes, structured asset destruction through inflation, asset stripping through mergers and acquisitions, the promotion of levels of debt incumbency that reduced whole populations, even in the advanced capitalist countries, to debt peonage, to say nothing of corporate fraud, dispossession of assets (the raiding of pension funds and their decimation by stock and corporate collapses) by credit and stock manipula-

43. A. Roy, *Power Politics* (Cambridge, Mass.: South End Press, 2001).
44. P. Dicken, *Global Shift: Reshaping the Global Economic Map in the 21st Century* (New York: Guilford Press, 4th edition, 2003), chapter 13.

tions – all of these became central features of the capitalist financial system. The emphasis on stock values, that arose out of bringing together the interests of owners and managers of capital through the remuneration of the latter in stock options, led, as we now know, to manipulations in the market that brought immense wealth to a few at the expense of the many. The spectacular collapse of Enron was emblematic of a general process that dispossessed many of their livelihoods and their pension rights. Beyond this, we also have to look at the speculative raiding carried out by hedge funds and other major institutions of finance capital for these formed the real cutting edge of accumulation by dispossession on the global stage, even as they supposedly conferred the positive benefit for the capitalist class of "spreading risks."[45]

3. The management and manipulation of crises

Beyond the speculative and often fraudulent froth that characterizes much of neo-liberal financial manipulation, there lies a deeper process that entails the springing of "the debt trap" as a primary means of accumulation by dispossession.[46] Crisis creation, management and manipulation on the world stage has evolved into the fine art of deliberative redistribution of wealth from poor countries to the rich. By suddenly raising interest rates in 1979, Volcker raised the proportion of foreign earnings that borrowing countries had to put to debt-interest payments. Forced into bankruptcy, countries like Mexico had to agree to structural adjustment. While proclaiming its role as a noble leader organizing "bail-outs" to keep global capital accumulation stable and on track, the US could also open the way to pillage the Mexican economy through deployment of its superior financial power under conditions of local crisis. This was what the US Treasury/Wall Street/ IMF complex became expert at doing everywhere. Greenspan at the Federal Reserve deployed the same Volcker tactic several times in the

---

45. The importance of spreading risks through financial derivatives is stressed in Panitch and Gindin, "Global Finance and American Empire", *op. cit.*
46. Gowan, *The Global Gamble, op. cit.*

1990s. Debt crises in individual countries, uncommon during the 1960s, became very frequent during the 1980s and 1990s. Hardly any developing country remained untouched and in some cases, as in Latin America, such crises were frequent enough to be considered endemic. These debt crises were orchestrated, managed and controlled both to rationalize the system and to redistribute assets during the 1980s and 1990s. Wade and Veneroso capture the essence of this when they write of the Asian crisis (provoked initially by the operation of US-based hedge funds) of 1997–8:

> Financial crises have always caused transfers of ownership and power to those who keep their own assets intact and who are in a position to create credit, and the Asian crisis is no exception . . . there is no doubt that Western and Japanese corporations are the big winners . . . The combination of massive devaluations, IMF-pushed financial liberalization, and IMF facilitated recovery may even precipitate the biggest peacetime transfer of assets from domestic to foreign owners in the past fifty years anywhere in the world, dwarfing the transfers from domestic to US owners in Latin America in the 1980s or in Mexico after 1994. One recalls the statement attributed to Andrew Mellon: 'In a depression assets return to their rightful owners.'[47]

The analogy with the deliberate creation of unemployment to produce a pool of low wage surplus labor convenient for further accumulation is exact. Valuable assets are thrown out of use and lose their value. They lie fallow and dormant until capitalists possessed of liquidity choose to seize upon them and breath new life into them. The danger, however, is that crises might spin out of control and become generalized, or that revolts will arise against the system that creates them. One of the prime functions of state interventions and of international institutions is to orchestrate crises and devaluations in ways that permit accumulation by dispossession to occur without sparking a general collapse or popular revolt. The structural adjustment

47. R. Wade and F. Veneroso, "The Asian Crisis: The High Debt Model versus the Wall Street-Treasury-IMF Complex," *The New Left Review* 228 (1998) pp. 3–23.

program administered by the Wall Street/Treasury/IMF complex takes care of the first while it is the job of the comprador neo-liberal state apparatus (backed by military assistance from the imperial powers) in the country that has been raided to ensure that the second does not occur. But the signs of popular revolt soon began to emerge, first with the Zapatista uprising in Mexico in 1994 and then later in the generalized discontent that emerged with the anti-globalization movement that cut its teeth in the revolt at Seattle.

4. State redistributions

The state, once transformed into a neo-liberal set of institutions, becomes a prime agent of redistributive policies, reversing the flow from upper to lower classes that had occurred during the era of social democratic hegemony. It does this in the first instance through pursuit of privatization schemes and cut-backs in those state expenditures that support the social wage. Even when privatization appears as beneficial to the lower classes, the long-term effects can be negative. At first blush, for example, Thatcher's program for the privatization of social housing in Britain appeared as a gift to the lower classes which could now convert from rental to ownership at a relatively low cost, gain control over a valuable asset and augment their wealth. But once the transfer was accomplished, housing speculation took over particularly in prime central locations, eventually bribing or forcing low income populations out to the periphery in cities like London and turning erstwhile working class housing estates into centers of intense gentrification. The loss of affordable housing in central areas produced homelessness for many and extraordinarily long commutes for those who did have low-paying service jobs. The privatization of the ejidos in Mexico which became a central component of the neo-liberal program set up during the 1990s, has had analogous effects upon the prospects for the Mexican peasantry, forcing many rural dwellers off the land into the cities in search of employment. The Chinese state has followed through a whole series of draconian steps in which assets have been conferred on a small elite to the detriment of the mass of the population.

The neo-liberal state also seeks redistributions through a variety of other means such as revisions in the tax code to benefit returns on investment rather than incomes and wages, promotion of regressive elements in the tax code (such as sales taxes), displacement of state expenditures and free access to all by user fees (e.g. on higher education) and the provision of a vast array of subsidies and tax breaks to corporations. The corporate welfare programs that now exist in the US at federal, state and local levels amount to a vast redirection of public moneys for corporate benefit (directly as in the case of subsidies to agribusiness and indirectly as in the case of the military-industrial sector), in much the same way that the mortgage interest rate tax deduction operates in the US as a massive subsidy to upper income home owners and the construction industry. The rise of surveillance and policing and, in the case of the US, incarceration of recalcitrant elements in the population indicate a more sinister role of intense social control. In the developing countries, where opposition to neo-liberalism and accumulation by dispossession can be stronger, the role of the neo-liberal state quickly assumes that of active repression even to the point of low-level warfare against oppositional movements (many of which can now conveniently be designated as "terrorist" so as to garner US military assistance and support) such as the Zapatistas in Mexico or the landless peasant movement in Brazil.[48]

In effect, reports Roy, "India's rural economy, which supports seven hundred million people, is being garroted. Farmers who produce too much are in distress, farmers who produce too little are in distress, and landless agricultural laborers are out of work as big estates and farms lay off their workers. They're all flocking to the cities in search of employment."[49] In China the estimate is that at least half a billion people will have to be absorbed by urbanization over the next ten years if rural mayhem and revolt is to be avoided. What they will do in the cities remains unclear, though, as we have seen, the vast physical infrastructural plans now in the works will go some way to absorbing the labor surpluses released by primitive accumulation.

The redistributive tactics of neo-liberalism are wide-ranging, so-

---

48. J. Stedile, "Brazil's Landless Battalions," in T. Mertes (ed.) *A Movement of Movements* (London: Verso, 2004).
49. Roy, *Power Politics, op. cit.*

phisticated, frequently masked by ideological gambits but devastating for the dignity and social well-being of vulnerable populations and territories. The global justice movement has done much to expose both the methods and the consequences of accelerating processes of accumulation by dispossession. The question then remains as to how opposition to these processes has been and might better be articulated.

Contradictions and oppositions within neo-liberalism

Neo-liberalism has spawned within itself an extensive oppositional culture. The opposition tends, however, to accept many of the basic propositions of neo-liberalism and focus on internal contradictions. It typically takes questions of individual rights and freedoms seriously and opposes them to the authoritarianism and frequent arbitrariness of political, economic and class power. It takes the neo-liberal rhetoric of improving the welfare of all and condemns neo-liberalism for failing in its own terms. Consider, for example, the first substantive paragraph of that quintessential neo-liberal program, the WTO agreement. The aim is:

> raising standards of living, full employment and a large and steadily growing volume of real income and effective demand, and expanding the production of and trade in goods and services while allowing for the optimal use of the world's resources in accordance with the objective of sustainable development, seeking both to protect and preserve the environment and to enhance the means for doing so in a manner consistent with their respective needs and concerns at different levels of economic development.[50]

Similar pious hopes can be found in World Bank pronouncements ("the reduction of poverty is our chief aim"). None of this sits easily with the actual practices that underpin the restoration or creation of class power.

The rise of opposition cast in terms of violations of human rights has been particularly spectacular since 1980 or so. Before then, Chandler

---

50. D. Rodrik, *The Global Governance of Trade: As If Development Really Mattered* (New York: United Nations Development Program, 2001) p. 9.

reports, a prominent journal such as *Foreign Affairs* carried not a single article on human rights.[51] Human rights issues came to prominence after 1980 and positively boomed after the events in Tiananmen Square and the end of the Cold War in 1989. This corresponds exactly with the trajectory of neo-liberalism and the two movements are deeply implicated in each other. Undoubtedly, the neo-liberal insistence upon the individual as the foundational and essentialist element in political-economic life does open the door to extensive individual rights activism. But by focusing on those rights rather than on the creation or re-creation of substantive and open democratic governance structures, the opposition cultivates methods that cannot escape the neo-liberal trap. The neo-liberal attachment to the individual is allowed to trump any social democratic concern for equality, democracy and social solidarities. The frequent appeal to legal action, for example, accepts the neo-liberal shift from parliamentary to judicial and executive powers. But it is costly and time-consuming to go down legal paths and the courts are in any case heavily biased towards ruling class interests both in terms of the class allegiance of the judiciary and the whole history of legal decisions which, in most bourgeois democracies, favor rights of private property and the profit rate over rights of equality and social justice. Law replaces politics "as the vehicle for articulating needs in the public setting." It is, Chandler concludes, "the liberal elite's disillusionment with ordinary people and the political process (that) leads them to focus more on the empowered individual, taking their case to the judge who will listen and decide."[52]

Since most needy individuals lack the financial resources to pursue their own rights, the only way in which this ideal can be articulated is through the formation of advocacy groups. The rise of advocacy groups and NGOs has, like rights discourses more generally, accompanied the neo-liberal turn and increased spectacularly since 1980 or so. The NGOs have in many instances stepped into the vacuum in social provision left by the withdrawal of the state from such activities. This amounts to a process

51. D. Chandler, *From Kosovo to Kabul: Human Rights and International Intervention* (London: Pluto Press, 2002) p. 89.
52. Chandler, *From Kosovo to Kabul, op. cit.*, p. 230.

of privatization by NGO. In some instances this seems to have helped accelerate further state withdrawal from social provision. NGOs thereby function as "trojan horses for global neoliberalism."[53] Furthermore, they are not democratic institutions. They tend to be elitist, unaccountable, and by definition distant from those they seek to protect or help, no matter how well-meaning they may be. They frequently conceal their agendas, and prefer direct negotiation with or influence over state and class power. They typically control their clientele rather than represent it. They claim and presume to speak on behalf of those who cannot speak for themselves, even define the interests of those they speak for (as if people are unable to do this for themselves), but the legitimacy of their status is always open to doubt.[54] When, for example, organizations agitate successfully to ban child labor in production as a matter of universal human rights, they may undermine economies where that labor is fundamental to survival. Without any viable economic alternative the children may be sold into prostitution instead (leaving yet another advocacy group to pursue the eradication of that). The universality presupposed in "rights talk" and the dedication of the NGOs and advocacy groups to universal principles sits uneasily with the local particularities and daily practices of political economic life.[55]

But there is another reason why this particular oppositional culture has gained so much traction in recent years. Accumulation by dispossession entails a very different set of practices from accumulation through the expansion of wage labor in industry and agriculture. The latter, which dominated processes of capital accumulation in the 1950s and 1960s, gave rise to an oppositional culture (such as that embedded in trade unions and working class political parties) that produced the social democratic compromise. Dispossession, on the other hand, is fragmented and particular – a privatization here, an environmental degradation there, a financial crisis of indebtedness somewhere else. It is hard to oppose all of this

53. T. Wallace, "NGO Dilemmas: Trojan Horses for Global Neoliberalism?" *Socialist Register* (London: Merlin Press, 2003) pp. 202–19. For a general survey of the role of NGOs see M. Edwards and D. Hulme (eds.) *Non-Governmental Organisations: Performance and Accountability* (London: Earthscan, 1995).
54. L. Gill, *Teetering on the Rim* (New York: Columbia University Press, 2000).
55. J. Cowan, M.-B. Dembour and R. Wilson (eds.) *Culture and Rights: Anthropological Perspectives* (Cambridge: Cambridge University Press, 2001).

specificity and particularity without appeal to universal principles. Dispossession entails the loss of rights. Hence the turn to a universalistic rhetoric of human rights, dignity, sustainable ecological practices, environmental rights, and the like, as the basis for a unified oppositional politics.

This appeal to the universalism of rights is a double-edged sword. It may and can be used with progressive aims in mind. The tradition that is most spectacularly represented by Amnesty International, Médecins Sans Frontières, and others cannot be dismissed as a mere adjunct of neo-liberal thinking. The whole history of humanism (both of the Western – classically liberal – and various non-Western versions) is too complicated for that. But the limited objectives of many rights discourses (in Amnesty's case the exclusive focus, until recently, on civil and political as opposed to economic rights) makes it all too easy to absorb them within the neo-liberal frame. Universalism seems to work particularly well with global issues such as climate change, the ozone hole, loss of biodiversity through habitat destruction, and the like. But its results in the human rights field are more problematic, given the diversity of political-economic circumstances and cultural practices to be found in the world. Furthermore, it has been all too easy to co-opt human rights issues as "swords of empire" (to use Bartholomew and Breakspear's trenchant characterization[56]). So-called "liberal hawks" in the U.S., for example, have appealed to them to justify imperialist interventions in Kosovo, East Timor, Haiti, and, above all, in Afghanistan and Iraq. They justify military humanism "in the name of protecting freedom, human rights and democracy even when it is pursued unilaterally by a self-appointed imperialist power" such as the US.[57] More broadly, it is hard not to conclude with Chandler that "the roots of today's human rights-based humanitarianism lie in the growing consensus of support for Western involvement in the internal affairs of the developing world since the 1970s." The key argument "is that international institutions, international and domestic courts, NGOs or ethics committees are better representatives of the people's needs than

---

56. A. Bartholomew and J. Breakspear, "Human Rights as Swords of Empire," *Socialist Register* (London: Merlin Press, 2003) pp. 124–45.
57. Ibid., p. 126.

are elected governments. Governments and elected representatives are seen as suspect precisely because they are held to account by their constituencies and, therefore, are perceived to have 'particular' interest, as opposed to acting on ethical principle."[58] Domestically, the effects are no less insidious. The effect is to narrow "public political debate through legitimizing the developing decision-making role for the judiciary and unelected task forces and ethics committees." The political effects can be debilitating. "Far from challenging the individual isolation and passivity of our atomised societies, human rights regulation can only institutionalise these divisions." Even worse, "the degraded vision of the social world, provided by the ethical discourse of human rights, serves, like any elite theory, to sustain the self-belief of the governing class."[59]

The temptation in the light of this critique is to eschew all appeal to universals as fatally flawed and to abandon all mention of rights as an untenable imposition of abstract ethics as a mask for the restoration of class power. While both propositions deserve to be seriously considered, I think it unfortunate to abandon this field to neo-liberal hegemony. There is a battle to be fought not only over which universals and what rights shall be invoked in particular situations but also over how universal principles and conceptions of rights shall be constructed. In this the critical connection forged between neo-liberalism as an evolution of a particular set of political-economic practices and the increasing appeal to universals, ethical principles and rights of a certain sort as a foundation for moral and political legitimacy should alert us. The Bremer decrees impose a certain conception of rights upon Iraq. At the same time they violate the Iraqi right to self-determination. "Between two rights," Marx famously commented in his chapter on struggles over the length of the working day, "force decides." If class restoration entails the imposition of a distinctive set of rights, then resistance to that imposition entails struggle for entirely different rights.

The positive sense of justice as a right has, for example, been a powerful provocateur in political movements: struggles against injustice have powerfully animated movements for social change. The

---

58. Chandler, *From Kosovo to Kabul, op. cit.*, p. 27; p. 218.
59. Ibid., p. 235.

problem, of course, is that there are innumerable concepts of justice to which we may appeal. But analysis shows that certain dominant social processes throw up and rest upon certain conceptions of justice and of rights. To challenge those particular rights is to challenge the social process in which they inhere. Conversely, it proves impossible to wean society away from some dominant social process (such as that of capital accumulation through market exchange) to another (such as political democracy and collective action) without simultaneously shifting allegiance from one dominant conception of rights and of justice to another. The difficulty with all idealist specifications of rights and of justice is that they hide this connection. Only when they come to earth in relation to some social process do they find social meaning.[60]

Consider, for example, the case of neo-liberalism. Rights cluster around two dominant logics of power – that of the territorial state and that of capital.[61] Consider, first, state powers. However much we might wish rights to be universal, it requires the protection of the state apparatus to enforce those rights. If political power is not willing, then notions of rights remain empty. Rights in this instance are fundamentally derivative of and conditional upon citizenship. The territoriality of jurisdiction then becomes an issue. This cuts both ways. Difficult questions arise because of stateless persons, migrants without papers, illegal immigrants and the like. Who is or is not a "citizen" becomes a serious issue defining principles of inclusion and exclusion within the territorial specification of the national or local state. How the state exercises sovereignty with respect to rights is itself a contested issue, but there are limits placed on that sovereignty (as China is discovering) by the rules embedded in neo-liberal capital accumulation. Nevertheless, the nation state, with its monopoly over legitimate forms of violence, can in Hobbesian fashion define its own bundle of rights and of interpretations of rights and be only loosely bound by international conventions. The US, for one, insists on its right not to be held accountable to crimes against humanity as defined in the international arena at the same time as it insists

60. D. Harvey, "The Right to the City," forthcoming in R. Scholar (ed.) *Divided Cities* (Oxford Amnesty Lectures).
61. Harvey, *The New Imperialism, op. cit.*

that war criminals from elsewhere be brought to justice before the very same courts whose authority it denies in relation to its own citizens.

To live under neo-liberalism also means to accept or submit to that liberal bundle of rights necessary for capital accumulation. We live, therefore, in a society in which the inalienable rights of individuals (and, recall, corporations are defined as individuals before the law) to private property and the profit rate trump any other conception of inalienable rights you can think of. Defenders of this regime of rights plausibly argue that it encourages "bourgeois virtues," without which everyone in the world would be far worse off. These include individual responsibility and liability, independence from state interference (which often places this regime of rights in severe opposition to those defined within the state), equality of opportunity in the market and before the law, rewards for initiative and entrepreneurial endeavors, care for oneself and one's own, and an open market place that allows for wide-ranging freedoms of choice of both contract and exchange. This system of rights appears even more persuasive when extended to the right of private property in one's own body (which underpins the right of the person to freely contract to sell his or her labor power as well as to be treated with dignity and respect and to be free from bodily coercions such as slavery) and the right to freedom of thought, of expression and of speech. Let us admit it: these derivative rights are appealing. Many of us rely heavily upon them. But we do so much as beggars live off the crumbs from the rich man's table. Let me explain.

I cannot convince anyone by philosophical argument that the neo-liberal regime of rights is unjust. But the objection to this regime of rights is quite simple: to accept it is to accept that we have no alternative except to live under a regime of endless capital accumulation and economic growth no matter what the social, ecological or political consequences. Reciprocally, endless capital accumulation implies that the neo-liberal regime of rights must be geographically expanded across the globe by violence (as in Chile and Iraq), by imperialist practices (such as those of the World Trade Organization, the IMF and the World Bank) or through primitive accumulation (as in China and Russia) if necessary. By hook or by crook, the inalienable rights of private property and the profit rate will be universally established. This is precisely what Bush means when he says the US dedicates itself to extend the sphere of liberty and freedom across the globe.

But these are not the only set of rights available to us. Even within the liberal conception as laid out in the UN Charter there are derivative rights such as freedoms of speech and expression, of education and economic security, rights to organize unions, and the like. Enforcing these rights would have posed a serious challenge to the hegemonic practices of neo-liberalism. Making these derivative rights primary and the primary rights of private property and the profit rate derivative would entail a revolution in political-economic practices of great significance. There are also entirely different conceptions of rights to which we may appeal – of access to the global commons or to basic food security, for example. "Between equal rights force decides" and political struggles over the proper conception of rights moves center stage to how possibilities and alternatives get represented, articulated and eventually born forward into transformative political-economic practices. The point, as Bartholomew and Breakspear argue, "is to recuperate human rights politics as part of a critical cosmopolitan project aimed explicitly against imperialism" and, I would add, neo-liberalism itself.[62] We will, however, return to this question by way of conclusion.

The neo-conservative response

Reflecting on the recent history of China, Wang suggests that:

> On the theoretical level, such discursive narratives as 'neo-Author-itarianism,' 'neoconservatism,' 'classical liberalism,' market extremism, national modernization . . . all had close relationships of one sort or another with the constitution of neoliberalism. The successive dis-placement of these terms for one another (or even the contradictions among them) demonstrate the shifts in the structure of power in both contemporary China and the contemporary world at large.[63]

62. Bartholomew and Breakspear, "Human Rights as Swords of Empire", *op.cit.*, p. 140.
63. Wang Hui, *China's New Order, op. cit.*, p. 44.

In its authoritarianism, militarism and hierarchical sense of power, neo-conservatism is entirely consistent with the neo-liberal agenda of elite governance and mistrust of democracy. From this standpoint neo-conservatism appears as a mere stripping away of the veil of author-itarianism in which neo-liberalism sought to envelope itself. But neo-conservatism does propose distinctive answers to one of the central contradictions of neo-liberalism. If "there is no such thing as society but only individuals" as Thatcher initially put it, then the chaos of individual interests can easily end up prevailing over order. The anarchy of the market, of competition and of unbridled individualism (individual hopes, desires, anxieties and fears; choices of lifestyle, of sexual habits and orientation, modes of self-expression and behaviors towards others) generate a situation that seems increasingly ungovern-able. It may even lead to a breakdown of all bonds of solidarity and a condition verging on social anarchy and nihilism.

In the face of this, some degree of coercion appears inevitable to restore order. The neo-conservatives prefer and emphasize militarization as an antidote to the chaos of individual interests. They are therefore far more likely to highlight threats, real or imagined, both at home and abroad, to the integrity and stability of the nation. In the US this entails triggering what Hofstadter refers to as "the paranoid style of American politics" in which the nation is depicted as besieged and threatened by enemies from within and without.[64] This style of politics has had a long history in the US and it rests on the cultivation of a strong sense of nationalism. Anti-communism was the central focus for this throughout the twentieth century (though anarchism and fear of China and of immigrants have also played their role in the past). Neo-conservatism is not new, therefore, and since World War II it has found a particular home in a powerful military-industrial complex that has a vested interest in permanent militarization. But the end of the Cold War posed the question of where the threat to US security was coming from. Radical Islam and China emerged as the top two candidates externally and dissident internal movements (the Branch Dravidians incinerated at Waco, militia movements that gave succor to

---

64. R. Hofstadter, *The Paranoid Style in American Politics and Other Essays* (Cambridge, Mass.: Harvard University Press, 1996 edition).

the Oklahoma bombing, the riots that followed the beating of Rodney King in Los Angeles, and finally the disorders that broke out in Seattle in 1999) had to be targeted internally by stronger surveillance and policing. The very real emergence of the threat from radical Islam during the 1990s that culminated in the events of 9/11 finally came to the fore as the central focus for the declaration of a permanent "war on terror" that demanded militarization at both home and abroad to guarantee the security of the nation. While, plainly, some sort of police/military response was called for to the threats revealed by the two attacks against the World Trade Center in New York, the arrival in power of neo-conservatives guaranteed an overarching and in the judgment of many an overreaching response in the turn to extensive militarization at home and abroad.

While neo-conservatives are all too willing to exercise coercive power, they still recognize, however, that some degree of consent is necessary. Neo-conservatism therefore seeks to restore a sense of moral purpose, some higher order values that will form the stable center of the body politic. Its aim is to control thereby the blatant contradiction between authoritarianism and individual freedoms within the neo-liberal ethos and to counteract the dissolving effect of the chaos of individual interests that neo-liberalism typically produces. It in no way departs from the neo-liberal agenda of a construction or restoration of a dominant class power. But it seeks legitimacy for that power through construction of a climate of consent around central moral values. This immediately poses the question of which moral values shall be central. It would, for example, be entirely feasible to appeal to the liberal system of human rights as embedded in the US Bill of Rights: after all, the aim of human rights activism, as Mary Kaldor argues, "is not merely intervention to protect human rights but the creation of a moral community."[65] But this would be inconsistent with the turn to militarization.

In the US the moral values that became central to the neo-conservative movement can best be understood as a logical outcome of the particular coalition that was built in the 1970s between elite class and business interests intent on restoring their class power and an electoral base among the "moral majority" of the disaffected white working class.

65. Chandler, *From Kosovo to Kabul, op. cit.*, p. 223.

The moral values centered upon cultural nationalism, moral righteousness, Christianity (of a certain evangelical sort), family values and right to
life issues, and on antagonism to the new social movements (feminism,
gay rights, affirmative action, environmentalism and the like). While this
alliance was mainly tactical under Reagan, the domestic disorder of the
Clinton years forced the moral values argument to the top of the agenda
in the republicanism of Bush the younger. It now forms the core of the
moral agenda of the neo-conservative movement.

The consolidation of this ideology has implications both domestically
and internationally. On the international stage, the trumpeting of the
superiority of "American values" and their presentation as "universal
values" for all of humanity is unavoidable. This makes it appear as if the
US is waging a "crusade" (which it is) for "civilized values" (which it
supposedly represents) on the world stage. The nationalism involved in
US behavior on the global stage becomes blatant and the sense of a moral
crusade affects everyday diplomacy particularly with respect to the
Israeli–Palestinian conflict, which the Christian right in the US, with
its strong belief in Armageddon, sees as fundamental to its own destiny.
The sense of moral superiority within the US provokes antagonism
towards the rest of the world at the same time as it closes down the
possibility of open dialogue and persuasive negotiation at home. The
neo-conservative turn of the Bush administration creates a very different
climate in world geopolitical relations to that pursued under the multi-
cultural neo-liberalism of the Clinton presidency.

But it would be wrong to see this neo-conservative turn as excep-
tional or peculiar to the US, even though there are special elements at
work in the US that may not be present elsewhere. Within the US this
assertion of moral values relies heavily upon appeals to ideals of nation,
religion, history, cultural tradition, and the like, and these ideals are by
no means confined to the US. The rise of nationalist sentiment in Japan
and China, for example, has been marked in recent years, and in both
instances this can be seen as an antidote to the dissolution of former
bonds of social solidarity under the impact of neo-liberalism. Strong
currents of cultural nationalism are stirring within the old nation states
(such as France) that now constitute the European Union. Religion
and cultural nationalism provided the moral heft behind the Hindu

Nationalist Party's success in importing neo-liberal practices into India in recent times. The invocation of moral values in the Iranian revolution and the subsequent turn to authoritarianism has not led to total abandonment of neo-liberal practices there even though the revolution was aimed at the decadence of unbridled market individualism. A similar impulse lies behind the long-standing sense of moral superiority that pervades countries like Singapore and Japan in relationship to what they see as the "decadent" individualism and the shapeless multiculturalism of the US. The case of Singapore is particularly instructive. It has combined neo-liberalism in the market place with draconian coercive and authoritarian state power while invoking moral solidarities based on ideals of a beleaguered island state (after its ejection from the Malaysian federation), of Confucian values, and most recently of a distinctive form of the cosmopolitan ethic suited to its current position in the world of international trade.

Clearly there are dangers in the consolidation of neo-conservative movements, each prepared to resort to draconian coercive practices while each espousing its own distinctive and supposedly superior moral values. What seems like an answer to the contradictions of neo-liberalism can all too easily turn into the problem. Indeed, the spread of neo-conservative power, albeit grounded very differently in different social formations, highlights the dangers of descent into competing perhaps even warring nationalisms, if not the clash of civilizations that someone like Huntington erroneously sees as inevitable on the world stage. If there is an inevitability it arises solely out of the turn to neo-conservatism rather than out of eternal truths concerning civilizational differences. The "inevitability" can therefore easily be rebuffed by turning away from neo-conservative solutions and seeking out other alternatives to confront if not supplant entirely the contradictions of neo-liberalism. It is to this issue that we now turn.

Alternatives

Our task is both to understand the world and, as Marx long ago argued, to change it. But if no social order can achieve changes that are not already latent within its existing condition and if we cannot hope to make our history and our geography except under historical and geographical conditions handed down to us, then the task of critical engagement with the historical geography of neo-liberalism and the subsequent turn to neo-conservatism is to search within the present for alternative futures.

There are two major paths to such an end. We may examine the plethora of oppositional movements to neo-liberalism and seek to distill from them the essence of a broad-based oppositional program. Or we can resort to theoretical and practical analysis of our existing condition (of the sort I have engaged in here) to define alternatives. To take the latter path in no way presumes that existing oppositional movements are wrong or somehow defective in their understandings. By the same token, oppositional movements cannot presume that analytic findings are irrelevant to their cause. The task is to initiate dialogue between those taking both paths and thereby to deepen collective understandings of possibilities and feasible alternatives.

Neo-liberalism has spawned a swath of oppositional movements both within and outside of its compass. Many of these movements are radically different from the worker-based movements that dominated before 1980.[66] I say "many" but not "all." Traditional worker-based movements are by no means dead even in the advanced capitalist countries where they have been much weakened by the neo-liberal onslaught upon their power. In South Korea and South Africa vigorous labor movements arose during the 1980s and in much of Latin America working class parties are flourishing if not in power. In Indonesia a putative labor movement of great potential importance is struggling to be heard. The potentiality for labor unrest in China is immense though quite unpredictable. And it is not clear either that the mass of the working class in the US which has over this last generation consistently

66. B. Gills (ed.) *Globalization and the Politics of Resistance* (New York: Palgrave, 2001); T. Mertes (ed.) *A Movement of Movements* (London: Verso, 2004); W. Bello, *Deglobalization: Ideas for a New World Economy* (London: Zed Books, 2002); P. Wignaraja (ed.) *New Social Movements in the South: Empowering the People* (London: Zed Books, 1993); J. Brecher, T. Costello, and B. Smith, *Globalization from Below: The Power of Solidarity* (Cambridge, Mass.: South End Press, 2000).

voted against its own material interests for reasons of cultural nation-alism, religion and opposition to multiple social movements, will forever stay locked into such a politics by the machinations of Republicans and Democrats alike. Given the volatility, there is no reason to rule out the resurgence of worker-based politics with a strongly anti-neo-liberal agenda in future years.

But struggles against accumulation by dispossession are fomenting quite different lines of social and political struggle.[67] Partly because of the distinctive conditions that give rise to such movements, their political orientation and modes of organization depart markedly from those typical of social democratic politics. The Zapatista rebellion, for example, did not seek to take over state power or accomplish a political revolution. It sought instead a more inclusionary politics to work through the whole of civil society in a more open and fluid search for alternatives that would look to the specific needs of the different social groups and allow them to improve their lot. Organizationally, it tended to avoid avant-gardism and refused to take on the form of a political party. It preferred instead to remain a social movement within the state, attempting to form a political power bloc in which indigenous cultures would be central rather than peripheral. It sought thereby to accomplish something akin to a passive revolution within the territorial logic of state power.

The effect of all these movements has been to shift the terrain of political organization away from traditional political parties and labor organizing into a less focused political dynamic of social action across the whole spectrum of civil society. But what it lost in focus it gained in terms of relevance. It drew its strengths from embeddedness in the nitty-gritty of daily life and struggle, but in so doing often found it hard to extract itself from the local and the particular to understand the macro-politics of what neo-liberal accumulation by dispossession was and is all about. The variety of such struggles was and is simply stunning. It is hard to even imagine connections between them. They were and are all part of a volatile mix of protest movements that swept the world and increasingly grabbed the headlines during and after the 1980s. These movements and revolts were sometimes crushed with ferocious violence, for the most

67. Harvey, *The New Imperialism*, *op. cit.*, chapter 4.

part by state powers acting in the name of "order and stability." Elsewhere they produced inter-ethnic violence and civil wars as accumulation by dispossession produced intense social and political rivalries in a world dominated by divide and rule tactics on the part of capitalist forces. Client states, supported militarily or in some instances with special forces trained by the major military apparatuses (led by the U.S. with Britain and France playing a minor role) took the lead in a system of repressions and liquidations to ruthlessly check activist movements challenging accumulation by dispossession.

The movements themselves have produced a plethora of ideas regarding alternatives. Some seek to de-link wholly or partially from the overwhelming powers of neo-liberalism and neo-conservatism. Others seek global social and environmental justice by reform or dissolution of powerful institutions such as the IMF, the WTO and the World Bank. Still others emphasize the theme of "reclaiming the commons" thereby signaling deep continuities with struggles of long ago as well as with struggles waged throughout the bitter history of colonialism and imperialism. Some envisage a multitude in motion, or a movement within global civil society, to confront the dispersed and decentered powers of the neo-liberal order, while others more modestly look to local experiments with new production and consumption systems animated by completely different kinds of social relations and ecological practices. There are also those who put their faith in more conventional political party structures with the aim of gaining state power as one step towards global reform of the economic order. Many of these diverse currents now come together at the World Social Forum in an attempt to define their commonalities and to build an organizational power capable of confronting the many variants of neo-liberalism and of neo-conservatism. There is much here to admire and to inspire.

But what sorts of conclusions can be derived from an analysis of the sort here constructed? To begin with the whole history of the social democratic compromise and the subsequent turn to neo-liberalism indicates the crucial role played by class struggle in either checking or restoring class power. Though it has been effectively disguised, we have lived through a whole generation of sophisticated class struggle on the part of the upper strata in society to restore or, as in China and Russia, to construct an overwhelming class power. The further turn to neo-conservatism is illustrative of the lengths to which that class will go and the strategies it is prepared to deploy in order to preserve and enhance its powers. And all of this occurred in decades when many progressives were theoretically persuaded that class was a meaningless category and when those institutions from which class struggle had hitherto been waged on behalf of the working classes were under fierce assault. The first lesson we must learn, therefore, is that if it looks like class struggle and acts like class struggle then we have to name it for what it is. The mass of the population has either to resign itself to the historical and geographical trajectory defined by this overwhelming class power or respond to it in class terms.

To put it this way is not to wax nostalgic for some lost golden age when the proletariat was in motion. Nor does it necessarily mean (if it ever should have) that there is some simple conception of the proletariat to which we can appeal as the primary (let alone exclusive) agent of historical transformation. There is no proletarian field of utopian Marxian fantasy to which we can retire. To point to the necessity and inevitability of class struggle is not to say that the way class is constituted is determined or even determinable in advance. Class movements make themselves though not under conditions of their own choosing. And analysis shows that those conditions are currently bi-furcated into movements around expanded reproduction in which the exploitation of wage labor and conditions defining the social wage are the central issues and movements around accumulation by dis-possession in which everything from classic forms of primitive accu-mulation through practices destructive of cultures, histories and environments to the depredations wrought by the contemporary forms of finance capital are the focus of resistance. Finding the organic link between these different class movements is an urgent theoretical and practical task. But analysis also shows that this has to occur in an historical-geographical trajectory of capital accumulation that is based in increasing connectivity across space and time but marked by deepening uneven geographical developments. This unevenness must be understood as something actively produced and sustained by processes of capital accumulation, no matter how important the signs may be of residuals of past configurations set up in the cultural landscape and the social world.

But analysis also points up exploitable contradictions within the neo-liberal and neo-conservative agendas. The gap between rhetoric (for the benefit of all) and realization (the benefit of a small ruling class) increases over space and time and the social movements have done much to focus on that gap. The idea that the market is about competition and fairness is increasingly negated by the facts of extraordinary monopolization, centralization and internationalization of corporate and financial power. The startling increase in class and regional inequalities both within states (such as China, Russia, India and Southern Africa) as well as internationally poses a serious political problem that can no longer be swept under the rug as something "transitional" on the way to a perfected neo-liberal world. The more neo-liberalism is recognized as a failed utopian project masking a successful project for the restoration of class power, the more it lays the basis for a resurgence of mass movements voicing egalitarian political demands and seeking economic justice, fair trade and greater economic security.

The rise of rights discourses under neo-liberalism also presents opportunities as well as problems. Even appeal to the conventional liberal notions of rights can form a powerful "sword of resistance" from which to critique neo-conservative authoritarianism, particularly given the way in which "the war on terror" has everywhere (from the US to China and Chechnya) been deployed as an excuse to diminish civil and political liberties. The rising call to acknowledge Iraqi rights to self-determination and sovereignty is a powerful weapon with which to check US imperial designs. But alternative bundles of rights can also be defined. I argued elsewhere for a bundle of rights to include the right to life chances, to political association and "good" governance, for control over production by the direct producers, to the inviolability and integrity of the human body, to engage in critique without fear of retaliation, to a decent and healthy living environment, to collective control of common property resources, of future generations, to the production of space, to difference and rights inherent in our status as species beings.[68] The

---

68. D. Harvey, *Spaces of Hope* (Edinburgh: Edinburgh University Press, 2000), chapter 12.

critique of endless capital accumulation as the dominant process that shapes our lives entails critique of those specific rights – to individual private property and the profit rate – which inhere in that process and vice versa. To propose a different bundle of rights carries with it, therefore, the obligation to specify a dominant social process within which such rights can be inherently embedded.

A similar argument can be made with respect to the neo-conservative search for a moral highground for its authority and legitimacy. Ideals of moral community and of a moral economy are not foreign to the left historically and many of the movements against accumulation by dispossession are actively articulating the construction of alternative social relations in moral economy terms. Morality is not a field to be defined solely by a reactionary religious right mobilized under the hegemony of a media and articulated through a political process dominated by corporate money power. The restoration of ruling class power under a welter of confusing moral arguments has to be confronted. The so-called "culture wars" – however misguided some of them may have been – cannot be sloughed off as some unwelcome distraction (as some on the traditional left argue) from class politics. Indeed, the rise of moral argument among the neo-conservatives attests not only to the fear of social dissolution under an individualizing neo-liberalism but also to the broad swaths of moral repugnance already in motion against the alienations, anomie, exclusions, marginalizations and environmental degradations produced in a neo-liberal world. The transformation of that moral repugnance into cultural and then political resistance is one of the signs of our times that need to be read correctly rather than shunted aside. The organic link between such cultural struggles and the struggle to roll back the overwhelming consolidation of class power calls for theoretical and practical exploration.

But it is the profoundly anti-democratic nature of neo-liberalism backed by the authoritarianism of the neo-conservatives that should surely be the main focus of political struggle. The democratic deficit in nominally "democratic" countries such as the US is now enormous.[69] Political representation is there compromised and corrupted by money

---

69. "Task Force on Inequality and American Democracy", *American Democracy*, *op.cit.* paints a devastating picture.

power. Basic institutional arrangements are seriously biased. Senators from twenty seven states with less than twenty percent of the population have more than half the votes to determine legislative agendas while the blatant gerrymandering of congressional districts to advantage whoever is in power is deemed constitutional by a judicial system increasingly packed with political appointees with a neo-conservative bias. Institutions with enormous power, like the Federal Reserve, are outside of any democratic control whatsoever. Internationally the situation is even worse since there is no accountability let alone democratic control over institutions such as the IMF, the WTO and the World Bank, while NGOs can also operate without democratic input or oversight no matter how well-intentioned their actions.

To bring back the demands for democratic governance and for economic, political and cultural equality and justice is not to suggest some return to a golden past since the meanings in each instance have to be re-invented to deal with contemporary conditions and potentialities. The meaning of democracy in ancient Athens has little to do with the meanings we must invest it with today in circumstances as diverse as Sao Paulo, Johannesburg, Shanghai, Manila, San Francisco, Leeds, Stockholm and Lagos. But the stunning point here is that right across the globe, from China, Brazil, Argentina, Taiwan, Korea as well as South Africa, Iran, India, Egypt, the struggling nations of Eastern Europe as well as in the heartlands of contemporary capitalism, there are groups and social movements in motion that are rallying to reforms expressive of some version of democratic values.[70]

US leaders have, with considerable public support, projected upon the world in general the idea that American neo-liberal values are universal and supreme and that such values matter since they are the heart of what civilization is about. The world is in a position to reject that imperialist gesture and refract back into the heartland of neo-liberal capitalism and neo-conservatism a completely different set of values: those of an open democracy dedicated to the achievement of social equality coupled with economic, political and cultural justice.

---

70. This is, for example, an argument to which Wang Hui, *China's New Order*, *op. cit.* frequently returns in the case of China.

NOTES TOWARDS A THEORY OF UNEVEN GEOGRAPHICAL DEVELOPMENT

Notes towards a theory of uneven geographical development

David Harvey

Preamble

The theory of uneven geographical development needs further development. The extreme volatility in contemporary political economic fortunes across and between spaces of the world economy (at all manner of different scales) cry out for better theoretical interpretation. The political necessity is just as urgent since convergence in well-being has not occurred and geographical as well as social inequalities within the capitalist world appear to have increased in recent decades. The promised outcome of poverty reduction from freer trade, open markets and "neo-liberal" strategies of globalization has not materialized. Environmental degradations and social dislocations have also been unevenly distributed. Simultaneously, the uneven geographical development of oppositional movements to neo-liberalism creates both opportunities and barriers in the search for alternatives.

There is nothing new, of course, about uneven geographical development within capitalism or, for that matter, within any other mode of production. There are, moreover, several overlapping ways of thinking about it:

1) Historicist/diffusionist interpretations treat the political economic development of the advanced capitalist countries (the West) as the

engine of capitalism that entrains all other territories, cultures and
places into paths of economic, political, institutional and intellectual
progress. Uneven geographical development is interpreted as the
product of a differentiated diffusion process from the center that leaves
behind residuals from preceding eras or meets with pockets of resistance towards the progress and modernization that capitalism promotes. "Backwardness" (the term is highly significant) arises out of an
unwillingness or an inability (in racist versions considered innate, in
environmentalist versions seen as naturally imposed, and in culturalist
versions understood in terms of the weight of historical, religious etc.
traditions) to "catch up" with the dynamics of a western-centered
capitalism, usually portrayed as the highpoint of modernity or even of
civilization. Whole populations, cultures and territories are thereby
presumed to be incapable of shaping their own history let alone of
influencing developments elsewhere. Occasionally some place "sees
the light" (e.g. Japan and more recently much of East and Southeast
Asia) and forges ahead. But the rest of the world lives in "the waiting
room of history." There are conservative, liberal and Marxist versions
of this historicist/diffusionist argument.

2) Constructivist arguments focus on the "development of underdevelopment." The exploitative practices of capitalism backed by the
political, military and geopolitical activities of the most powerful nation
states engaging in imperialist, colonial or neo-colonial exploitation of
territories and whole populations and their cultures lie at the root of the
uneven geographical development. Differential patterns of exploitation
(of populations, resources, lands) result. Indigenous strengths and
cultural specificities stand to be undermined or destroyed by these
forces over large tracts of the globe. While the forces at work exploiting
the territory are basically external, indigenous comprador classes may
collaborate and sometimes acquire enough power to retain a portion of
the fruits of exploitation within the territory and build a good life for
themselves. There are conservative (in the tradition of Edmund Burke),
liberal (human rights) and Marxist (e.g. dependency theory, unequal
exchange, development of underdevelopment and production of
space) versions of this constructivist approach.

3) Environmentalist explanations go back at least to Montesquieu

and Rousseau. Though their reputation became sullied by association with racism and doctrines of (usually) European cultural superiorities, the thread of argument that attributed developmental differences to underlying environmental conditions never disappeared. In recent years, under the pressure of many "green" arguments regarding natural limits, environmental capacities and differential exposure to health problems and diseases (e.g. the impact of malaria in tropical regions) we have seen a "respectable" revival of such thinking in the works of Jared Diamond and Jeffrey Sachs. More benign versions take up the ways in which human adaptations to variegated environmental possibilities underlie territorial specializations, divisions of labor and the creation of distinctive regional ways of life albeit within a framework of continuous capital accumulation. Again, there are conservative, liberal, bioregionalist, and now Marxist/Green versions of this argument.

4) Geopolitical interpretations see uneven geographical development as an unpredictable outcome of political and social struggles between territorially organized powers operating at a variety of scales. These powers can be organized as states or blocs of states but struggles also occur between regions, cities, communities, local neighborhoods, turfs, etc. In past times organic metaphors were frequently deployed in which the survival of the fittest territorial polity depended upon competitive strength. More recent versions drop the crude social Darwinism and concentrate on the play of power politics (military, political, economic) and competition between territorially based organizations for wealth, power, resources and qualities of life on the global stage. Imperialist versions stress the abilities of states or collections of states to extract surpluses from the rest of the world and reduce much of the world to a subservient division of labor convenient to the needs of hegemonic power(s). There is room for a good deal of contingency in geopolitical interpretations. Accidents of history (localized social movements, cultural norms, political shifts, revolutions) and geography (resources, human capital, prior investments) can all play a role in defining the forms of struggle as well as their outcomes. Emancipatory struggles over national self-liberation for oppressed peoples contrast, for example, with struggles to maintain the hegemony of some dominant power or powers within global capitalism.

Again, there are conservative, liberal and Marxist-realist versions of this argument.

There are plainly many overlaps between these different approaches. But which basic line of argument is taken becomes important because it sets limits on the terrain of possible debate about the role of uneven geographical development within capitalism and circumscribes what can be legitimated and justified from the standpoint of political action. Under (1), for example, primitive accumulation and the radical transformation of nature can be seen as necessary evils, a stage to be gone through in order to break with tradition, superstition, religion etc. en route to a better kind of society. Capitalism and even imperialism can be seen as progressive movements in world history and if a society has not gone through that then socialists or other "progressive" forces have to do the nasty work (e.g. Soviet dispossession of the Kulaks). Under (2) it is hard to construct the same legitimacy for capitalism and its cognate forms of colonialism, neo-colonialism and imperialism. The exploitative and destructive practices are inevitably cast in a negative light. Movements for autonomy (such as de-linking from the global economy) and national liberation coupled with a refusal to engage in certain kinds of environmental transformation are seen as progressive forms of resistance. Under (3) the question of environmental constraints (even imperatives) to uneven geographical development becomes much more compelling, even as the distinction between natural and built environments becomes less and less easy to sustain. Judgments are cast and politics defined in ecological terms and those terms limit possibilities. In extreme versions of the argument, environmental constraints provide norms to which uneven geographical development should conform. Under (4) we are more likely to assume that competitive struggle between political entities is inevitable: the only interesting question is who comes out on top where and why (with historical and geographical "accidents" often playing a key role).

In their more extreme forms it is impossible to reconcile these different arguments. I start, however, with the idea that the arguments are not necessarily mutually exclusive; each has something significant to say about uneven geographical development. This poses the danger that we merely end up with an eclectic and incoherent mish-mash of ideas. I prefer to brave that danger. In what follows, therefore, I shall explore the potential interplay of all of these themes in a relational way. The aim is to identify a "unified" field theory of uneven geographical development. I place the term "unified" in quotation marks because, as will become apparent, the sense of unification to be achieved is very different from reductionist or even organicist conceptions of how theory might be constructed. For purposes of simplification, I focus exclusively on how uneven geographical development works under capitalism.

The structure of argument

Any theory of uneven geographical development must be simple enough to aid comprehension and complex enough to embrace the nuances and particularities that call for interpretation. I construct the argument around four radically distinct conditionalities that have different epistemological statuses. A unified field theory rests on combining these conditionalities. The combination turns out to be difficult and I do not claim to have solved all of its problems. I suggest instead a mode of approach that points the way towards the possibility of general theory. The four conditionalities are:

1) The material embedding of capital accumulation processes in the web of socio-ecological life.
2) Accumulation by dispossession (a generalization of Marx's concept of "primitive" or "original" accumulation under which pre-existing assets are assembled – as labor powers, money, productive capacity or as commodities – and put into circulation as capital).
3) The law-like character of capital accumulation in space and time.
4) Political, social and "class" struggles at a variety of geographical scales.

How, then, might these elements be combined into a unified theory? The answer in part depends upon the conception of "theory" being advanced. If theory is construed as a clean logical structure specified in direct propositional terms with law-like statements neatly derived from fundamental abstract categories, then the materials I assemble here would be incapable of theorization. But I have a somewhat looser conception of theory in mind: one that acknowledges the power and importance of certain processes that are specifiable independently of each other but which can and must be brought together in a dynamic field of interaction. This implies the construction of arguments about how the web of life and accumulation by dispossession and accumulation through expanded reproduction work together and how the dynamics of political and class struggles power continuous changes in capitalism's uneven geographical development.

While the proof of this approach must await its execution, I think it useful to lay out two preliminary points which have been crucial in guiding my own thinking. The first concerns the way in which Marx formulated the relationship between the abstract and the concrete in his work. To comprehend this would require a full-length exposition in its own right, so I confine myself to the following observations. Dialectics, and in particular that version of it which stresses internal relations, is perpetually negotiating the relation between the particular and the universal, between the abstract and the concrete. There is, in Marxian theory for example, no such thing as abstract labor outside of the multiple concrete activities of production and exchange which give rise to it, while the concrete is, as Marx observed, a concentration of so many different determinations that it can never be reduced to a mere particular manifestation of the abstract. Agents (and all of us have agency of some kind) make their own way but do so, to paraphrase a well-known Marxist adage, not under conditions of their own making nor with results that are free of multiple determinations deriving from the actions of others. Much of social theory has been taken up with considerations of this sort: how to relate individual agency (however that is understood) to the evolution of social structures and vice versa. Dialectics avoids the more mechanistic and reductionist versions of this problem and permits the issue to be approached theoretically in an open and fluid way. I shall, in what follows, rely heavily on this dialectical way of assembling together the abstract and the concrete, the universal and the particular.

The second point rests on the conception of space to be deployed (see next chapter). This is crucial since the very term uneven geographical development is predicated upon some conception of what spatiality is all about. The tendency in much of social theory is either to exclude spatiality altogether from its purview as an unnecessary complication or to treat of it as a simple and immutable container within which social processes occur. Under either of those presumptions a general theory of uneven geographical development of the sort I have in mind becomes impossible. The best that could be articulated is a study of how the laws of accumulation produce uneven development within a predetermined spatial structure. But in recent years many geographers backed by the philosophical arguments of Lefebvre and others have come to view spatiality in a different light, as actively produced and as an active moment within the social process. Treating of space relationally and relatively rather than as an absolute framework for social action, it becomes possible to see the ways in which capital accumulation, for example, creates not only spaces but different forms of spatiality (through such moves as the organization of financial markets in cyberspace). This whole idea opens up the prospect for theories of the production of space and spatiality. This is, as Neil Smith long ago insisted, a necessary precondition for the construction of any general theory of uneven geographical development.[1] I examine it in greater detail in the next chapter.

The material embedding of social processes in 'the web of life'

Uneven geographical developments reflect the different ways in which different social groups have materially embedded their modes of sociality into the web of life, understood as an evolving socio-ecological system. The system is open and dynamic and, clearly, there are abundant examples of unintended consequences of social action as well

1. N. Smith, *Uneven Development: Nature, Capital and the Production of Space* (Oxford: Basil Blackwell, Reprint Edition, 1990).

as all manner of environmental shifts that occur simply because of what Whitehead called "the perpetual search for novelty" within nature (including human nature). Geographers, anthropologists, sociologists, economists, historians of various kinds, political commentators and many more have produced in fact a vast body of work relevant to understanding such processes and outcomes. The archive of studies of how daily life is lived within the web of life around the world is therefore immense. The problem is to find a way to make sense of diverse, particular and often quite idiosyncratic geographical variations in relation to more general processes of capital accumulation, social struggle and environmental transformation. This means integrating particular studies into some more general theory of the uneven geographical development of capitalism.

Capitalist activity is always grounded somewhere. Diverse material processes (physical, ecological as well as social) must be appropriated, used, bent and re-shaped to the purposes and paths of capital accumulation. Conversely, capital accumulation has to adapt to and in some instances be transformed by the material conditions it encounters. Theory has to address two issues: first, the rules of capital circulation and accumulation need to be specified and, secondly, a methodology must be established to track how those rules get tangibly expressed and actively re-shaped through socio-ecological processes.

The conventional approach to the second question is to insist that case studies be "theoretically informed". What this all too often means, however, is an introductory and concluding chapter in which the works of major theoreticians are in the forefront of argument, separated by a case study in which it is often hard to discern even a trace of influence of any of the theoretical work appealed to at the beginning and the end. The issue of how theoretical work might in turn be informed and advanced by case study work is rarely if ever addressed. What sometimes happens instead is that theory is judged inadequate, when the real question should be how to advance the theory. This conventional approach to the question arises I suspect because "theory" is all too often understood as a bundle of stationary, already fully specified arguments and propositions, ready-made to be applied to and tested against the "real" world. This positivist approach to theory testing is a problem. Theory should be understood instead as an evolving structure of argument sensitive to encounters with the complex ways in which social processes are materially embedded in the web of life. My aim here, therefore, is to talk through the problematics of a general theory of uneven geographical development that both loosens up the conception of how theory in general works at the same time as it tightens the dialectical integration of theoretical work and the tangible practices of historical-geographical materialism.[2]

These difficulties are exacerbated by the habit of many influential and thoughtful practitioners such as Braudel and Habermas, to view the abstractions of capital accumulation as somehow "outside of" daily life, apart from what some like to call "the lifeworld." Braudel, for example, conceives of capitalism as the top layer of a three-tiered structure. The lowest layer is constituted by "material life" defined as that "stratum of the non-economy, the soil into which capitalism thrusts its roots but which it can never really penetrate." Above this layer:

> comes the favored terrain of the market economy, with its many horizontal communications between different markets: here a degree of automatic coordination usually links supply, demand and prices. Then alongside, or rather above this layer, comes the zone of the anti-market, where the great predators roam and the law of the jungle operates. This – today as in the past, before and after the industrial revolution – is the real home of capitalism.[3]

Braudel sees everyday material life before 1800 as being lived in local ways that are only marginally affected by capitalism. At one point he does express some doubt as to whether this continued to be true after the arrival of the railroads in the nineteenth century. There are

2. The closest I have come to laying out the general principles of what I mean by "historical-geographical materialism" is in D. Harvey, *Justice, Nature and the Geography of Difference* (Oxford: Basil Blackwell, 1996).
3. F. Braudel, *Capitalism and Material Life, 1400–1800*, translated by M. Kochan (London: Weidenfeld and Nicolson, 1973); *Afterthoughts on Material Civilization and Capitalism*, translated by P. Ranum (Baltimore: Johns Hopkins University Press, 1977). The actual quote is cited in G. Arrighi, *The Long Twentieth Century* (London: Verso, 1994) p. 10.

certainly areas of the world even today where it would be entirely
reasonable to argue that the macro processes of capitalism merely cast a
shadow over daily life. But this is less and less the case. Consider the
role of Enron – a quintessential "predator" in Braudel's terms – in the
California energy crisis. The shortages and the rapidly rising price of
electricity as well as the indirect budgetary consequences affected
everyone in California and beyond. Consider the effects of fiscal crises
and structural adjustment policies in Mexico, Argentina, Mozambique,
Indonesia, Thailand and Korea (just to name a few); the daily lives of
almost everyone in those countries were profoundly altered. As the
financial crisis progressed in Southeast Asia in 1997–8, for example:

> unemployment soared, GDP plummeted, banks closed. The un-
> employment rate was up fourfold in Korea, threefold in Thailand,
> tenfold in Indonesia. In Indonesia, almost 15 percent of males
> working in 1997 had lost their jobs by August 1998, and the
> economic devastation was even worse in the urban areas of the
> main island, Java. In South Korea, urban poverty almost tripled,
> with almost a quarter of the population falling into poverty; in
> Indonesia, poverty doubled.[4]

The riots and violence (mainly visited on ethnic Chinese) that
followed in Indonesia, for example, tore apart a lot of the social fabric.
No place or person was immune, though the effects were clearly
stronger in some places than in others. Innumerable social struggles
have also erupted against capitalism (the Zapatista movement against
NAFTA, the large number of documented anti-IMF riots, for example). It is impossible, I conclude, to sustain the view that capitalism
has only a shadowy relation to daily life or that the adjustments and
adaptations that occur in daily life are irrelevant for understanding how
capital accumulation is working on the global stage. Braudel's formulation is inappropriate to our contemporary world.

Polanyi, for his part, saw what he called a gradual "disembedding" of
the market economy from the social system. By the time "the great
transformation" (the rise of the market economy) was complete, the

---

4. J. Stiglitz, *Globalization and Its Discontents* (New York: Norton, 2002) p. 97.

logic of commodification (of land, labor and money, none of which are actually produced as commodities) and of capital accumulation had been imposed upon social life as a set of fictions and abstractions. The problem, as Polanyi saw it, was to re-embed capital accumulation and market relations in a regulatory and institutional framework that would curb its excesses while sustaining some of its virtues (such as freedom of choice and decentralized decision making). Polanyi's argument is not, of course, that the circulation of capital is materially outside of the web of social and ecological life, but that the abstractions that drive it are separated from the broader logic that would derive from social and ecological processes taken as a whole.[5] This leads to a host of potentially destructive consequences within the web of life, particularly for the environment and for labor. This seems to me a more solid formulation. The danger, however, is that we construe the abstractions and fictions of capitalism's logic as the property of some mystical external force – "capital" – outside of the "web of life" and immune to materialist influences when they should be characterized, rather, as the product of a perverse and limiting logic arising out of the institutional arrangements constructed at the behest of a disparate group of people called capitalists. Capitalists adapt to new conditions: indeed one of the more outstanding things about capitalist historical geography is precisely its flexibility and adaptability. New institutional arrangements are constantly being constituted in response to the circumstances of material embedding of capital circulation within the web of life. Capitalism has modified its behaviors, for example, through its encounters with environmental limits and constraints. What Marx called the "elastic" powers of capital in its quest for surplus value have to be incorporated into the theoretical argument.

Other theorists postulate the existence of protected spaces (dubbed "heterotopic" by Foucault) within which daily life and affective relations can function without being dominated by capital accumulation, market relations and state powers. Habermas turns to Husserl's concept of "the lifeworld" understood as that sphere of both non-human and human thought and action outside of the economic, technical and bureaucratic

5. K. Polanyi, *The Great Transformation* (Boston: Beacon Press, 1957 edition).

rationality given in the concepts of capital and the state. In Habermas's case, there is a manifest desire to retain a humanism in which personal passions and concerns, individual moral and aesthetic judgements, communicative ethics and dialogue carry their own distinctive and autonomous meanings. Formulations of this type guard a space against the overwhelming power of "capital logic" theory and the seemingly anti-humanistic stance which that logic dictates.[6] I am sympathetic to that overall aim but think it erroneous and self-defeating to presume the existence of some heterotopic or segregated "lifeworld" space insulated from (even if in the long run in danger of being penetrated and swamped by) capitalist social relations and conceptions. To accept such a division between "lifeworld" and "system" entails abandoning everything Marx taught us regarding the principles of historical materialist enquiry. Marx, after all, sought a critical knowledge of everyday life. His method entailed "a ruthless criticism of everything existing." Though Marxism has fallen victim on occasion to its own abstractions, the fundamental line of enquiry must center on the dialectical relations between abstractions and concrete events.

If it is invidious to view daily life and the lifeworld as something "outside of" the circulation of capital, then we have to concede that everything that now occurs in the workplace and in the production-consumption process is somehow caught up within capital circulation and accumulation. Almost everything we now eat and drink, wear and use, listen to and hear, watch and learn comes to us in commodity form and is shaped by divisions of labor, the pursuit of product niches and the general evolution of discourses and ideologies that embody precepts of capitalism. It is only when daily life has been rendered totally open to the circulation of capital and when political subjects have their vision almost entirely circumscribed by embeddedness in that circulation that capitalism can function with affective meanings and legitimacy as its support. Under such circumstances the body becomes "an accumulation strategy" and we all of us live our lives under the sign of that condition.[7] This

6. J. Habermas, *The Theory of Communicative Action, Volume 2, Lifeworld and System: A Critique of Functionalist Reason* (Boston: Beacon Press, 1985).
7. D. Harvey, *Spaces of Hope* (Edinburgh: Edinburgh University Press, 2000).

is now true even for those populations trying to subsist on less than $2 a day and who are often viewed and treated as if they are disposable and redundant populations.

It is undeniable, of course, that capitalism has promoted and evolved institutional frameworks and specializations of function that promote the development of discourses so abstract as to be opaque to the mass of the population. This is particularly true of the financial system with its derivatives and hedge-funds, its junk bonds and currency futures, its complex rules of behavior and the gyrations in valuation of assets that seem to make it a world of its own, the focus of immense speculative energies seemingly unrelated to the world of material production and consumption. The task for critical enquiry, is to penetrate to the underlying meaning of such phenomena and to explore their ramifications for daily life. How to do this is the big question. Gramsci's insights are here of considerable relevance:

> The active man in the mass has a practical activity, but has no clear theoretical consciousness of his practical activity, which nonetheless involves understanding the world in so far as it transforms it. His theoretical consciousness can indeed be historically in opposition to his activity. One might almost say that he has two theoretical consciousness (or one contradictory consciousness): one which is implicit in his activity and which in reality unites him with his fellow workers in the practical transformation of the real world; and one superficially explicit or verbal, which he has inherited from the past and uncritically absorbed. But this verbal conception is not without consequences. It holds together a specific social group, it influences moral conduct and the direction of will, with varying efficacity but often powerfully enough to produce a situation in which the contradictory state of consciousness does not permit any action, any decision or any choice, and produces a condition of moral and political passivity.[8]

"Common sense," Gramsci argued, is:

8. A. Gramsci, *Selections from The Prison Notebooks*, translated by Q. Hoare and G. Nowell Smith (London: Lawrence and Wishart, 1971) p. 333.

> The conception of the world which is uncritically absorbed by the various social and cultural environments in which the moral individuality of the average man is developed. Common sense is not a single unique conception, identical in time and space . . . Its most fundamental characteristic is that it is a conception which, even in the brain of one individual, is fragmentary, incoherent and inconsequential, in conformity with the social and cultural position of those masses whose philosophy it is.

This bundle of beliefs held in common contrasts with "good sense" that connects life activity with understanding in a profound and critical way:

> Each one of us changes himself, modifies himself to the extent that he changes and modifies the complex relations of which he is the hub. In this sense the real philosopher is and cannot be other than, the politician, the active man who modifies the environment, understanding by environment the ensemble of relations which each of us enters to take part in. If one's own individuality is the *ensemble* of those relations, to create one's personality means to acquire consciousness of them and modify ones own personality means to modify the *ensemble* of these relations.[9]

Given the fetishisms that attach to and the opacities that mask processes of capital circulation and accumulation, we cannot expect anything other than "common sense" conceptions of the world to regulate the conduct of daily life. The disjunctions and cognitive dissonances are important. There is no way we can expect the rules and laws of capital accumulation to enter into the socio-ecological world in an unmediated way. But by the same token, this means that the activities of capital circulation and accumulation are refracted through actual discursive practices, understandings and behaviors (including the passivity and "common sense" that Gramsci identifies). These mediations shape the uneven geographical development of capitalism in important ways. But this then brings us back full circle

9. Ibid., p. 419, p. 352.

for if it is indeed the case, as I shall later argue, that territorial competition plays a crucial role in the progress of capital accumulation, then the uneven and disparate structures of "common sense" that arise within the different spaces of capitalism play a shaping if not constitutive role. If, for example, "common sense" in Silicon Valley is founded in beliefs with respect to rugged entrepreneurial individualism and venture capitalism then the relative success of that region versus the staid sociality of the British shires or the religious intensity of Karachi is not hard to predict. The geography of "common sense" appears to me to be the proper subject of cultural geography and anthropology.

Lefebvre likewise provides key insights. His project is to liberate Marxism from its dogmatism and to integrate an understanding of "everyday life" into Marxian theory. "The method of Marx and Engels" he insists:

> consists precisely in a search for the link which exists between what men think, desire, say and believe for themselves and what they are, what they do. This link always exists. It can be explored in two directions. On the one hand, the historian or the man of action can proceed from ideas to men, from consciousness to being – i.e. towards practical, everyday reality – bringing the two into confrontation and thereby achieving *criticism of ideas by action and realities* . . . But it is equally possible (to take) real life as the point of departure in an investigation of how the ideas which express it and the forms of consciousness which reflect it emerge. The link, or rather the network of links between the two poles will prove to be complex . . . In this way we can arrive at a *criticism of life by ideas* which in a sense extends and completes the first procedure.[10]

Lefebvre identifies a series of critical points where this operation can be conducted. He proposes a critique of (a) individuality (private consciousness); (b) of mystifications (mystified consciousness); (c) of money (fetishism and economic alienation); (d) of needs (psychological and moral alienation); (e) of work (alienation of the worker); and (f) of

---

10. H. Lefebvre, *Critique of Everyday Life*, Volume One, translated by J. Moore, (London: Verso, 1991) p. 145.

freedom (the power over nature and human nature). Lefebvre high-lights the necessity of *critique* as the epistemological underpinning for any attempt to integrate everyday material concerns into some broader framework. Lefebvre takes us from the field of mere description of the everyday (paralleling Gramsci's "common sense") to a consideration of the possibility of its transformation (searching for Gramsci's "good sense"). The critique of everyday life entails the construction of a set of possibilities for its transformation, taking us from the passivity that Gramsci describes to one of revolutionary action. Socialism, for Lefebvre, is nothing less than the transformation of everyday life. But these transformations are occurring willy-nilly all around us. The world is therefore replete with possibilities. But the possibilities are seized upon unevenly, depending upon the degree to which the politics of good sense trump the passivity that common sense typically imparts. The uneven geographical development of everyday life is the product of processes whereby we make ourselves and our world through transformative activities, with respect to both discursive understandings and daily-life practices.

My sense from reading Gramsci and Lefebvre and reflecting on numerous specific case studies is that it is entirely possible to construct a mode of what might be called "bottom-up theorizing." Let me be clear that I am not here advocating a return to some version of the inductive method in which a whole series of empirical enquiries provide raw materials for the extraction of synthetic generalizations that can then take on the role of theoretical propositions. Marx's method of descent from the surface appearance of particular events to the ruling abstractions underneath is very different. It entails viewing any particular event set as an internalization of fundamental underlying guiding forces. The task of enquiry is to identify these underlying forces by critical analysis and detailed inspection of the individual instance. I stand, in short, to learn far more about the urban process under capitalism by detailed reconstruction of how a particular city has evolved than I would from collection of empirical data sets from a sample of one hundred cities. From this perspective we see that all case studies necessarily internalize theory construction. "Doing theory" is, therefore, an inevitable concomitant of all forms of historical-geographical materialist enquiries. Through activities of this sort it then becomes possible to re-formulate and advance whatever general theory (such as that which Marx advances in *Capital*) we have at hand. The final chapter of any case study should therefore be about how the case study has advanced the theory and with what general effects.

We also need here to examine more closely the metabolic relations between capital accumulation and "nature" since it is often and plausibly argued that this puts us on a qualitatively different terrain with respect to theory construction. Certainly, as Smith argues, an understanding of uneven geographical development depends upon first understanding "the production of nature" through capitalistic activities.[11] Physical and ecological conditions vary greatly across the surface of the earth. The temptation to homogenize the category "nature" (as often happens in philosophical debates) must be avoided. Nature should always be regarded as intensely internally variegated – an unparalleled field of difference. The possibility to mobilize and appropriate physical surpluses varies enormously from one environmental context to another and the geographical circulation of capital reflects that simple fact. But the possibilities also depend upon technologies, organizational forms, divisions of labor, wants, needs and desires as well as our cultural predilections (including those articulated in "common sense"). This natural world is, furthermore, in perpetual flux, with anthropogenic influences looming larger and larger in scale and importance over time. The implications are legion. Paul Burkett puts it this way:

> Nature's capacity to absorb or adjust to the human production process is itself largely determined by the combined qualities of the material objects, physical forces, and life forms constituting particular ecosystems and the terrestrial biosphere as a whole. The myriad forms, and the spatial and temporal unevenness, of human impacts on the biosphere can only be understood in terms of the qualitative variegation and differential resiliency of nature within and across ecosystems. Of course, uneven and differentiated human ecological

11. Smith, *Uneven Development, op. cit.*

impacts also implicate the specific features of human development, as compared to other species. The social division of labor, in particular gives the level and qualitative differentiation of human production a peculiar momentum relative to extra-human nature.[12]

In transforming our environment we necessarily transform ourselves. This is Marx's most fundamental theoretical point concerning the dialectics of our metabolic relation to nature. "The antithesis between nature and history is created," Marx and Engels observed, only when "the relation of man to nature is excluded from history."[13] And if that relation is seen as dialectical, as a matter of internal relations, then the particularity-universality problem is directly confronted. On the ecological side, therefore, we have to understand how the accumulation of capital works through ecosystemic processes, re-shaping them and disturbing them as it goes. Energy flows, shifts in material balances, environmental transformations (some of them irreversible) have to be brought thoroughly within the picture. But the social side cannot be evaded as somehow radically different from its ecological integument. There is, as I argued in *Justice, Nature and the Geography of Difference*, nothing unnatural about New York City.[14] The circulation of money and of capital have to be construed as ecological variables every bit as important as the circulation of air and water. The concept of embeddedness in "the web of life" understood both in ecological and social terms therefore becomes crucial to the theorization of uneven geographical development. This is the kind of work that political ecology has embarked upon with significant results.

This dialectic has unfolded, however, without us being particularly cognizant of the ways we re-make ourselves. Even when there was some collective sense of how "the mastery of nature" (just to take one example) might contribute to human enlightenment and emancipation, the unintended consequences of human actions have been so vast

12. P. Burkett, *Marx and Nature: A Red and Green Perspective* (New York: Palgrave Macmillan, 1999) p. 21.
13. K. Marx and F. Engels, *Collected Works, Volume 5* (New York: International Publishers, 1975) p. 55.
14. Harvey, *Justice, Nature and the Geography of Difference, op. cit.*, p. 186.

and unexpected as to disrupt and in some instances even reverse some of our most cherished hopes. The unexpected outcomes feed our Frankenstein fears instead. All the problematics posed by environmentalism here loom large. The question of how capital accumulation works through the physical, chemical and biological processes that surround us becomes a compelling issue for critical work.

This becomes even more evident when we insert the word "built" in front of the word "environment." For the city as the noted urban sociologist Robert Park once remarked, is:

> man's most consistent and on the whole, his most successful attempt to remake the world he lives in more after his heart's desire. But, if the city is the world which man created, it is the world in which he is henceforth condemned to live. Thus, indirectly, and without any clear sense of the nature of his task, in making the city man has remade himself.[15]

We have, however, largely surrendered our own individual right to make the city after our heart's desire to the rights of property owners, landlords, developers, finance capitalists and the state. These are the primary agents that shape our cities for us and thereby shape us. We have abrogated our right to make ourselves to the rights of capital to make us through the passive acceptance or mindless embrace of the restructuring of daily life by the projects of capitalist class interests. If the results are not too prepossessing, then we have to reclaim our right to change them. Critical and dialectical method is vital to understand not only where we have been and how we have been re-made but also to understand where we might go and what we might collectively aspire to become.

The rich variety encountered in the how, why and where of the material embedding of social processes in the web of life must be an integral consideration in any attempt to construct a general theory of uneven geographical development. But at this point in our history, we do not approach this question empty-headed as to the general nature of

15. R. Park, *On Social Control and Collective Behavior* (Chicago: Chicago University Press, 1967 edition) p. 3.

the social process of capital accumulation. And it is to these matters that
we now turn.

Accumulation/devaluation by dispossession

All societies generate surpluses (defined as use values greater than those
required for immediate consumption) for survival. The more elaborate
the social system the more important and necessary the surpluses
become. Favorable natural conditions make surplus generation easier
but the class appropriation and centralization of surpluses depends
entirely upon political developments and the formation of class powers.
Appropriating surpluses produced by others or seeking command over
those natural conditions that permit the easy production of surpluses
has been a long-standing human practice. The only interesting questions are: who gets to do the appropriating, how much surplus can be
appropriated and how does the surplus get used? Theocracies (like
Ancient Egypt or the Incas), imperial states (like Rome and China),
urban plutocracies or democracies (Classical Greece and Venice),
feudal orders of various kinds, all depended upon surplus generation
and appropriation by a certain kind of political and class power.
Political, military and social struggles over surplus appropriation and
use have been both frequent and often violent.

The rise of the capitalist class did not depend initially upon its
capacity to generate surpluses. It rested, rather, upon its ability to
appropriate them, treat them as their own private property and launch
them into circulation in search of further surpluses. While commerce,
banking and usury provided opportunities to gain profit, capitalism as a
social system eventually came to depend upon the formation of a
proletariat and the employment of wage labor. Surplus generation
could then be assured internally within the system on a continuous
basis. Traces of attempts to work in such a way can be found in many
areas of the world at different times (particularly in Arab and Chinese
trading areas and around the Mediterranean) but in each instance the
rise of a bourgeoisie to a hegemonic position was thwarted by other
class powers (usually religious or state-based). For capitalism to become

dominant as a social system required that the bourgeoisie emerge victorious over other class forces controlling surpluses. How and why this occurred in Europe (and then only in certain parts) is a matter of controversy but that it did first occur there on a self-sustaining basis is not in doubt. The ability of merchants to roam the high seas and appropriate surpluses from around the world (sometimes peaceably, sometimes violently) and to concentrate them in Europe (thus making cities and states heavily dependent upon their activities) coupled with the dissolution of feudal powers (the transformation of serfs into wage laborers) and the appropriation of church domains in certain areas had much to do with it. It was in part the weakness of other class powers controlling the surplus that accounted for the unique conditions for the bourgeois conquest of power in Europe.

Once the European–centered capitalist system was formed, struggles over the appropriation, control and use of surpluses did not cease. Indeed the evidence points to continuous struggle in part to preserve bourgeois and capitalist class power (against, for example, the threats of socialism, communism or various forms of theocratic reaction). Even more important, however, has been the unceasing search to extend capitalist power to territories, sectors and domains in which surpluses (or favorable natural conditions for the production of surpluses) were not yet incorporated into the circulation of capital. Accumulation through dispossession is to be construed therefore as a necessary condition for capitalism's survival. This proposition (a generalized version of Luxemburg's argument that continuous imperial expansion is a necessary condition for the survival of capitalism) requires more detailed specification.[16]

To begin with, surpluses come in a variety of forms. Natural resources and other conditions in nature provide for the possibility of rapid surplus production so that open access to and control over resource rich sites becomes a shadow form of accumulation through appropriation. The perpetual search for natural resources of high

---

16. R. Luxemburg, *The Accumulation of Capital*, translated by A. Schwartzschild (New York: Monthly Review Press, 1968); see also Chapter 1 (above) and D. Harvey, *The New Imperialism* (Oxford: Oxford University Press, 2003); *A Short History of Neoliberalism* (Oxford: Oxford University Press, 2005).

quality that can be pillaged for surplus and surplus value production has therefore been a key aspect to the historical geography of capitalism. To the degree that these resources and resource complexes are unevenly distributed so a certain kind of uneven geographical development results built around conditions of, say, agricultural productivity or the presence of oil reserves. Land, use values that can be commodified, money commodities (gold), labor powers (including skills), cultural artifacts and local customs, social networks, and the like, provide more direct targets for appropriative activities. All of these are geographically differentiated and located and their appropriation therefore depends upon spatial strategies to gain access to and command over them.

Consider, for example, the appropriation of cultural histories as commodities to be consumed through tourism. The search for monopoly rents on the part of capital creates a premium on the commodification of phenomena that are in other respects unique, authentic and therefore non-replicable.[17] Pillaging of cultural histories, the collection and exhibition of unique artefacts (museums of all sorts) and the marketing of places as somehow unique environments has in recent years become big business. But for this to occur entails the wholesale appropriation by capital of all manner of things which it has little or nothing to do with creating. Furthermore this appropriation carries over into the realms of individual creativity (consider how the music industry has pillaged regional traditions as well as new genres of music generated out of the conditions of daily life (such as hiphop and rap)). Thus is the creativity embedded in the web of life appropriated by capital and circulated back to us in commodity form so as to allow the extraction of surplus value. This is appropriation of creativity and affective cultural forms by capital and not direct creation by capital itself.

Dispossession occurs in a variety of ways. External coercion by some superior power (merchants, states, colonial powers, multinationals, etc.) entails the penetration of some pre-existing social order and geographical terrain to the advantage of that power. The long history

17. D. Harvey, "The Art of Rent: Globalization, Monopoly and the Commodification of Culture", *Socialist Register* (2002) pp. 93–110.

of merchant capitalism as well as colonial, neo-colonial and imperialist endeavors is fundamentally of this sort. Robbing the world of use values has a long history in the bourgeois pantheon of infamous deeds. But it would be wrong to conclude that this is the only or even the dominant form. Once the power of capital circulation and its cognates (eventually technological and military superiority) had been clearly demonstrated, there was a standing temptation for subordinate groups to collaborate with external capitalist power to gain control of their own surpluses. Whole social formations that had suffered mightily from the depredations of capital could conclude that if they could not beat capitalism they may as well join it. State and factional class powers in non-capitalist social formations can mobilize surpluses internally (sometimes by force) and circulate them as capital through world trade. There is a long history of such activity as countries as diverse as Japan during the Meiji restoration and, more recently, China have used state powers to mobilize their own internal surpluses for circulation as capital in the world market. In other instances (such as South Korea or Japan after World War II) it is the combination of external influences and internal powers that accumulated surpluses for capitalist develop-ment. A whole series of "comprador" bourgeois and capitalist class factions have sprung up using powers of appropriation in different places (with or without access to state violence) as part of the network of global capitalism. Ambitious factions, often working at the local level, can extract surpluses (sometimes through vicious means) at the expense of fellow citizens as part of a strategy of self-insertion into the world market. Success or failure, determined in the rough waters of international competition, is never guaranteed and this year's success story can easily become next year's failure (as in the recent case of Japan). Uneven geographical development is a corollary of such diverse processes. Clearly, there is a great deal of contingency in the when, where and how of accumulation through dispossession. But the general proposition still stands: that there is an aggregate degree of accumula-tion through dispossession that must be maintained if the capitalist system is to achieve any semblance of stability. Uneven geographical development through dispossession, it follows, is a corollary of capitalist stability.

But this tells only part of the story of accumulation through dispossession. The other half looks more closely at the cannibalization of assets that goes on within the capitalist system itself as factions (such as finance capital) seize opportunities to appropriate assets of others (such as farmers or industrialists) or as territories or regional configurations of capital (cities, regions, states) seek to acquire or destroy the assets of rivals through commercial competition and/or geopolitical maneuvers (including military interventions and disruptions). Acquisition through mergers and asset stripping are likewise common enough capitalist practices. The destruction of assets (as in the case of the destruction of a very well-developed Indian handicraft textile industry to make way for cheap British exports of cotton goods in the nineteenth century) can be just as important as their absorption into new configurations of uses. During capitalist crises, we have argued, capital gets devalued which means that surplus values and eventually the surpluses that lie behind them are diminished or destroyed. Crises of devaluation provide multiple opportunities to acquire assets "on the cheap" and those with the power to ride out the crises can emerge much enriched. On the world stage this has meant, as Arrighi shows, major geographical and also scalar shifts in the hegemonic center of capital accumulation over time (moving from the Italian city states to the Netherlands to Britain and then to the United States). But crises also spark intense geopolitical rivalries and power struggles between factions and territories as to who is going to bear the brunt of devaluation and where. The aim of appropriating or controlling the surpluses of others is not, in this case, to absorb them into the circulation of capital but to have the power to devalue them and even destroy them (militarily if necessary) thus confining the impacts of devaluation to the places of others. Financial control through indebtedness is now the chief means for imposing the devaluation of capital elsewhere. We have to look no further than the structural adjustment programs of the International Monetary Fund for examples of how this works. Devaluation is, then, place-specific (witness what happened in Argentina after 2001). The patchy geographical effects of this across regions or states is registered as uneven geographical development.

Capital accumulation is necessarily materially grounded in the web of socio-ecological life. But capital accumulation is not only about the production and circulation of surpluses as surplus values. It is also about the appropriation of the assets of others. Any theory of uneven geographical development under capitalism must incorporate accumulation/devaluation through dispossession as a fundamental force if it is to be of any general validity and utility.

Capital accumulation in space and time

We have at hand a reasonably good approximation to a general theory of capital accumulation in space and time.[18] This theory operates on the presumption that original accumulation has already occurred and that a capitalist class and a proletariat have already formed; that a "facilitative state" enforcing certain institutional arrangements (law, contract, private property and individual juridical rights) is firmly in place; that the material world in which processes of accumulation occur has been rendered pliable and manipulable to capitalist ends. Capital accumulation is, furthermore, assumed to possess the following fundamental characteristics: (1) activity is expansionary and growth is accepted as both inevitable and good, (2) growth is sustained through the exploitation of living labor in production, (3) class struggle is endemic but not threatening, (4) technological change (or "progress") is inevitable and accepted as a good in itself, (5) the system is contradictory and inherently unstable (conditions of production of capital in

18. The account that follows is largely drawn from my own writings in D. Harvey, *The Limits to Capital* (Oxford: Basil Blackwell, 1982) and the relevant essays in *Spaces of Capital* (Edinburgh: Edinburgh University Press, 2001). For a critical appraisal of this work see N. Castree, J. Essletzbichler and N. Brenner (eds.) "Symposium: David Harvey's The Limits to Capital: Two Decades On," Antipode 36 (3) (2004) pp. 401–549. Other major contributions can be found in Smith, *Uneven Development, op. cit.*; E. Sheppard, T. Barnes and C. Pavlik, *The Capitalist Space Economy: Analytic Foundations* (New York: Routledge, 1990); M. Webber and D. Rigby, *The Golden Age Illusion: Rethinking Postwar Capitalism* (New York: Guilford, 1996); K. Cox (ed.) *Spaces of Globalization: Reasserting the Power of the Local* (New York: Guilford Press, 1997) and many others.

the workplace perpetually conflict with those of realization of capital in the market, for example), (6) crises are inevitable and are characterized by overaccumulation (a condition in which surpluses of capital and labor exist side by side with seemingly no way to bring them together), and (7) if the surpluses cannot be somehow absorbed then they will be devalued (written down, sold at a loss or even physically destroyed). Overaccumulation crises can be at least temporarily relieved either by a temporal shift (the absorption of capital and labor surpluses in long-term projects such as large scale public works) or through a spatial fix (dispersing or exporting capital and labor surpluses into new and more profitable spaces).

How, then, can a more explicit theory of uneven geographical development be constructed internal to this general way of under-standing capital accumulation? The argument runs through a number of theoretical steps.

Market exchange

Bringing together labor power and means of production at a site of production and sending the finished commodity to consumers entails spatial movements of commodities that take time. Transport costs are incurred and this limits the spatial range over which exchange is economically possible. This is particularly important with respect to the daily flow of labor power between place of work and place of residence. The spatial range over which commodities can move depends upon transportation capacities and the means, cost and time taken. But in any given historical-geographical situation the spatial range and time taken are roughly known and a very specific spatio-temporal structure to capital accumulation arises.

The classical location theory of Lösch, Weber, and others would at first sight appear helpful here. The difficulty is that this theory – at least in Lösch's case – presumes an equilibrium arising out of rational trade-offs between rising transport costs over distance and corresponding diminution of demand. Profitable activity is limited to geographically specific market areas. But capitalism is about growth not stationary state equilibrium. The problem is to see how spatially confined market

structures evolve in relation to both growth and technological dynamism. Furthermore, commodities do not take themselves to market:
they are taken there by merchants. The constant probing of spatial
barriers and opening up of new spaces is their forte. When local
markets were restricted by high transport costs, as in the middle ages,
merchants became itinerant peddlers who sold their wares on the move
over vast areas. The prospect of buying cheap and selling dear has led to
the construction of all manner of different methods and means of
marketing. Wildly differing ranges of similar goods have arisen depending upon the forms taken by merchant capital and trade. In more
recent times much attention has properly been paid to commodity
chains, to social relations and structures within the market system, the
power of merchant capitalists (as monopsonists, for example) and how
these mediations not only facilitate transfers of commodities but also set
up innumerable points for the extraction of value and surplus value (as
processors, wholesalers, retailers all mediate the flows, employ wage
labor, and take their cut). Uneven geographical development is
produced by such means.

The coercive laws of spatial competition

Capitalist producers in competition with each other seek to gain
advantage and higher profits by adopting superior technologies and
organizational forms. This advantage is, however, temporary and
ephemeral since competitors will (unless prevented by monopoly
controls, patent laws and the like) catch up or even leapfrog over
into new technological/organizational mixes. From this we derive the
inevitability of technological and organizational dynamism within
capitalism. Production functions constantly change and the geographical landscape of capitalism becomes unstable. Capitalists occupying
superior locations likewise gain excess profits. This advantage is likely
to be temporary also for two reasons: other capitalists can find similarly
advantageous locations or, if the excess profits turn out to be relatively
permanent, then they may be "taxed away" by high land rents/prices:
the excess profits will by siphoned off by a landlord class. But the search
for excess profits generates a locational dynamism within production

that parallels technological and organizational dynamism. Trade-offs exist between these two ways of gaining competitive advantage (e.g. capitalists can stay with their old technologies in highly favored locations). The coercive laws of competition nevertheless produce perpetual instability within the geographical landscape of capitalism.

Geographical divisions of labor

Small pre-existing geographical differences, be it in natural resources or socially constructed endowments, get magnified and consolidated rather than eroded by free market competition. The coercive laws of competition push capitalists to relocate production to more advantageous sites and the special requirements of particular forms of commodity production push capitalists into territorial specializations. This can occur in a variety of ways. Besides the more obvious regional specializations in production due to different resource endowments, differences between constructed endowments (built environments for example) have effects. This brings the urban process into focus as central to the theory. But different sectors of the economy such as command and control functions, research and development, production, marketing and finance are organized differently and have their own distinctive locational requirements and spatial range (e.g. money can move much more easily over space, especially as credit, than commodities or production activities). Financial control can be and increasingly is located in one place while merchant activity and production occur elsewhere. Agglomeration economies (including those achieved through urbanization) generate a locational dynamic in which new production tends to be drawn to existing production locations. Much attention has been paid in recent years to the "self-organizing" dynamics of concentration and centralization of capital in space. Circular and cumulative causation within the economy then ensures that capital rich regions tend to grow richer while poor regions grow poorer. The tension between geographical centralization and dispersal is omnipresent within the geographical landscape.

Monopolistic competition

Monopoly is a foundational concept because (a) monopoly control over the means of production in the form of private property arrangements lies at the very basis of capitalism, (b) the end result of competition is likely to be monopoly (witness the incredible rise of monopoly and oligopoly powers in the recent period of neo-liberal dominance) and (c) capitalists seek out monopoly powers because this provides greater security, calculability, and allows for rational structures of exploitation. Conventional location theory correctly appeals to a theory of monopolistic competition because whoever controls the property rights at a particular location is a monopolist in absolute space and time.

In the past, high transport costs and other barriers to movement (tolls and tariffs) meant the existence of many local monopolies. In the early nineteenth century, for example, the local brewer, baker and candlestick maker were all protected from competition by high transport costs. By this measure, nineteenth century capitalism, though small scale and dispersed, was far less competitive than now. But as spatial barriers diminished so many local industries lost their monopoly privileges. They were forced to compete with producers in other locations, at first relatively close by and then with those further and further away. In recent years declining transport costs and reductions in barriers to trade (tariffs, etc.) have reduced if not eliminated the spatial and territorial aspects of monopolistic competition in many sectors (personal services being a major exception, though even here some service functions have been taken off-shore). Though the monopoly element due to spatial location has not entirely disappeared, capitalists have had to find different ways to construct and preserve their monopoly privileges (against the flood of products coming from China for example). The two major moves entail increasing centralization of capital and protection of technological advantages through patent laws and intellectual property rights. In both instances, the effect is to collect powerful forces of capital accumulation at key sites, such as so-called "global" cities. Activities in other spaces may then become subservient to these centralized powers. The visible hand (as Chandler calls it) of multinational corporations has consequently been of considerable if not greater importance in the uneven geographical development of capitalism relative to the hidden hand of the market.

Speed-up and the annihilation of space through time

There are strong incentives, both individually and collectively, to minimize the turnover time of capital and, as a consequence, we see many innovations designed to speed up production, marketing and consumption. Since distance is measured in terms of time and cost of movement, there is also intense pressure to reduce the frictions of distance by innovations in transportation and communications. The reduction in the cost and time of movement of commodities, people (labor power), money and information through what Marx called "the annihilation of space through time" is a basic law of capital accumulation. It has a notable presence within the historical geography of capitalism and underpins the production of uneven geographical development in many ways. One effect has already been noted: the systematic reduction over time of the element of monopolistic competition in space fixed by transport and communications costs. Any spatial arrangement achieved under one set of transport and communications relations (e.g. railroads and telegraph) will have to be changed to meet the conditions of any new set (e.g. air transport and the internet). Also, we must take account of the differential geographical mobilities of capital (as money, as commodities, as production activities) and of labor. The easier movement of money capital, for example, may create difficulties particularly for types of production that find it hard to move.

The general diminution in transport costs in no way disrupts the significance of territorial divisions and specializations of labor. Indeed, it makes for more fine-grained territorial divisions since small differences in production costs (due to raw materials, labor conditions, intermediate inputs, consumer markets, infrastructural or taxation arrangments) are more easily exploitable by highly mobile capital. Reducing the friction of distance, in short, makes capital more rather than less sensitive to local geographical variations. The combined effect of freer trade and reduced transport costs is not greater equality of power through the evolving territorial division of labor, but growing geographical inequalities.

Physical infrastructures (fixed capital embedded in the land) for production and consumption

Spatially fixed and immobile physical infrastructures of transport and communications systems (ports, airports, transport systems) are required in order to liberate other forms of capital and labor for easy spatial movement. Transport investments get drawn towards major centers of production, finance and commerce because that is where they are likely to be most profitable. A powerful centripetal force is felt as uneven geographical investments in transport systems feed further uneven geographical developments. Behind this lies a fundamental contradiction between fixity and movement within the theory of capital accumulation in space and time. Physical investments embedded in the land form necessary preconditions for processes of exchange, production and consumption. Very specific conditions regulate the circulation of capital in built environments (usually involving heavy reliance upon credit and debt-financing if not state expenditures on projects that capital would find it difficult or impossible to undertake). The path of such investments can easily run against the grain of standard circulation processes precisely because it works on a different spatio-temporal horizon compared to the standard form of capital circulation. Investments of this sort must cohere so that transport relations, working class housing, factories and offices, shopping malls and leisure places, institutions (hospitals, schools, etc.) hang together in physical space in reasonably coordinate and mutually accessible ways. The effect is to concentrate these investments geographically. This concentration entails the production of urbanization as a spatially-ordered physical framework within which capital accumulation can proceed.

Competition between different land uses, the power of land owners to extract rent from favored locations as well as the tendency for physical landscapes to become more sclerotic and less flexible with time, all tend to freeze patterns of uneven geographical development. Landed capital often requires heavy support from finance capital and/ or the state in order to elaborate and build projects that require adequate and continuous use over a considerable period of time if they are not to be devalued. Building a port facility to which no ships come entails devaluation of the capital sunk into that facility. Geographical fixity tends to increase, therefore, in the midst of the struggle to acquire greater geographical mobility for all the other factions of capital. Clearly, there is abundant opportunity here for tensions between factions of capital as well as for crises of devaluation in the built environment.

The production of regionality

Investments in the built environment effectively define regional spaces for the circulation of capital. Within these spaces, production, distribution, exchange and consumption, supply and demand (particularly for labor power), class struggle, culture and lifestyles hang together within an open system that nevertheless exhibits some kind of "structured coherence." Modes of consumption here become geographically differentiated according to concentrations of wealth and power (e.g. the immense concentration of wealth in Manhattan turns this into a very special market) and cultural differentiations can either be transformed or actively produced that generate niche markets. The differentiated world of consumer power and consumption preferences here enters in as a major determinant of uneven geographical development. Regional consciousness and identities, even affective loyalties, may build within this region and, when it is overlain by some apparatus of governance and state power, the regional space can evolve into a territorial unit that operates as some kind of defined space of collective consumption and production as well as political action. The collectivity can consolidate itself by assuming responsibility for embedding all manner of infrastructures in the land (highway systems, port facilities, water and sewage systems, etc.) and setting up multiple institutional supports (education and healthcare) that define a particular way of relating to capital accumulation as well as to the rest of the world.

A regional class alliance then typically emerges to establish a pattern of governance in which the stakes are fundamentally the economic health and well-being of the region rather than that of class. Landed capital (and developer capital) often takes the lead in "growth machine" politics but frequently finance capital is also heavily involved because of the heavy dependence of landed capital on the credit system. Here enters "growth machine politics", "urban entrepreneurialism" and "regional growth coalitions" and other structures of governance dedicated to improving the competitive strength of the region/territory vis-à-vis other regions/territories. Local bourgeoisies (small commercial enterprises, landowners, landlords) may offer popular support and frequently elements of the working class can be persuaded to join a local class alliance on the grounds that the welfare of the region will provide spillover benefits for them. The structure of local alliances is highly variable depending upon who takes the leadership role, what the project is and how it is articulated. Alliances can easily become exclusionary (e.g. anti-immigrant) as well as developmental and they can be fractured and conflict-ridden or comfortably hegemonic depending upon conditions. One of the great variables in uneven geographical development, therefore, is the nature and form of regional class alliance formation.

There are of course always forces at work that undermine regionality as structured coherence. Class alliances can dissolve or shift. Boundaries are porous and both capital and labor can migrate in and out (particularly in response to place-specific crises and devaluations). Revolutions in transport relations can shift patterns of integration and change the scale at which structured coherence might best be achieved. Resources can be exhausted or become diminished in significance because cheaper resources are opened up elsewhere. Past infrastructural arrangements and investments can be rendered obsolete by powerful currents of technological change. Class struggles can spill outwards and inwards and fragmentations wrought by conflicts within the governance structure can undermine political coherence (think of the long-standing problems of Northern Ireland as a site for capital accumulation). International pressures can likewise so affect the regional structure as to render its earlier coherence obsolete (as happened

in many older industrial regions with deindustrialization in the 1980s
and 1990s). Nevertheless there is abundant evidence that regionality is
always "under production" as well as "in the course of modification"
through capital accumulation. Further capital accumulation always has
to negotiate, confront and if necessary revolutionize the regional
structures it had earlier produced. Capitalism cannot exist without
engagements of this sort. The theory of uneven geographical development therefore has to acknowledge the power of these processes,
independent of any pre-existing proclivity to construct territorial
structures for other reasons.

The production of scale

The annihilation of space through time entails scalar transformations in
the spatio-temporal structuration of capital accumulation. It extends
the typical spatial range of goods, of financial flows as well as the
availability of information. It transforms the geography of labor
markets. Tensions between centralization and decentralization of
capital (e.g. of corporate organization), between geographical concentration and dispersal of activities are much in evidence. Territorial
divisions of labor, technologies and organizational forms and economies of likewise have impacts. How we understand the production of
scale under capitalism is a crucial question. It has been the focus of study
in recent years. One thing is clear: the dominant geographical scale at
which accumulation occurs has been changing over time. A hierarchy
of scales (often depicted as local, regional, national and global, though
these are arbitrary designations in themselves) exists through which the
circulation of capital works at the same time as it produces its own
distinctive scales of organization.

The scale of regionality that made sense at one time does not,
therefore, necessarily do so at another. Regional structures have to be
understood as inherently unstable at the same time as volatility of
capital and labor flows between them become endemic to the uneven
geographical development of capitalism. But this in turn requires that
we confront the whole issue of territorial administration (and particularly the state and its powers) as overlain upon the inherent tendency

towards the production of regionality through the circulation and accumulation of capital.

Territorial systems of political administration (the interventionist state)

Capitalism did not invent territorial administration. It seized hold of political-administrative structures and adapted, transformed and in some instances totally revolutionized them as it came to dominate as a political-economic system. If states had not existed, in short, capitalism would have had to invent them. In practice, the world has been reterritorialized by bourgeois power. In many instance this was achieved by carving out territorial administrative structures for colonial rule. While it is certainly true that the conveniences of colonial administration or the competing fantasies of colonial powers were by no means automatically consistent with commercial and capitalistic requirements, the resulting patchwork quilt of colonial territories, evolving with decolonization into independent states, served capital accumulation in a rough and ready fashion. The rise of the nation state in Europe and elsewhere, on the other hand, was a much more complicated affair in which the struggle of the bourgeoisie for political domination against non-capitalistic powers was partially fought out in terms of the territorial structure of administration. The control of the monetary, legal, military and ideological apparatus was crucial for capitalist economic activity to flourish. The unification of Italy and Germany contrasts, for example, with the break up of the older Austro-Hungarian and Ottoman Empires that were not organized along capitalistic lines.

Capitalist hegemonic power has steadily shifted scales over time from the Italian City States (like Venice and Genoa), through the intermediate organizational forms of Holland to Britain and, finally, to the United States. The most recent bout of capitalist globalization has been accompanied by strong currents of reterritorialization reflecting changing transportation and scale pressures. Organizations like the European Union, NAFTA, Mercosur, have become more salient at the same time as urban regions (like Catalonia) and in some instances even quasi-city states (Singapore and Hong Kong) have become vigorous centers of capitalist endeavor. While it would be erroneous to insist, as some now do, that traditional nation states have become irrelevant and powerless in relation to global capital, they have certainly become much more porous (particularly with respect to capital flow) and they have in some important respects changed their functions (mainly towards the neo-liberal goal of establishing a "good business climate" for investment as we saw in Chapter 1). In its neo-liberal configuration, the state functions more clearly now as an "executive committee of capitalist class interests" than at any other time in history.

Adequate territorial structures of administration and power are a necessary condition for the survival of capitalism. The difficulty is that territorial powers, once formed, become relatively fixed attributes of capitalism's geography and resist pressures for change. The tension between fixity and motion in the landscape of capitalism is re-emphasized because the state is about fixity rather than motion. But the state, as the lynch-pin of regionality, is the primary vehicle to assure the production of the collective preconditions for production, exchange and consumption. State administration is always therefore an active agent in capital circulation and accumulation. The "interventionist" state necessarily supercedes the "facilitative" state of liberal and neo-liberal theory. It also assumes a role in attempting to mediate or even resolve the chronic crisis tendencies of capitalism through fiscal and monetary policies.

The state as a political entity exists as a terrain of class struggle and class alliance formation. It must, if it is to function at all, be open to some form of democratic governance (however biased and limited). Capitalist class factions as well as other classes and social groups fight for their distinctive interests within a state political realm that is always unpredictable and prone to political/ideological instability. The result is uneven geographical development in everything from welfare arrangements to state economic policies and investment decisions. States and other political entities (such as cities and metropolitan governments) are also forced willy-nilly into competitive struggles with other entities for economic as well as political advantage. Since war and other forms of military pressure are useful tools ("diplomacy by other means" as the famous adage goes) then it follows that the military balance of power plays almost as important a role as economic power in preserving advantageous positions within the global economy. This leads us to consider, however, the inherent geopolitics of capitalism.

The geopolitics of capitalism

A central contradiction exists within capitalism between *territorial* and *capitalistic* logics of power. This contradiction is internalized within capital accumulation given the tension between regionality and territorial class alliance formation on the one hand and the free geographical circulation of capital on the other. By territorial logic, I mean the political, diplomatic and military strategies invoked and used by a terrritorially defined entity such as a state as it struggles to assert its interests and accumulate power in its own right. The capitalistic logic focuses on the ways in which economic power flows across and through continuous space, towards or away from territorial entities (such as states or regional power blocs) through the daily practices of production, trade, commerce, capital flows, money transfers, labor migration, technology transfer, currency speculation, flows of information, cultural impulses, and the like. The two logics are rather different. While they are not reducible to each other they are closely intertwined. To begin with, the motivations and interests of agents differ. The capitalist holding money capital will wish to put it wherever profits can be had and typically seeks to accumulate more capital. Politicians and statesmen typically seek outcomes that sustain or augment the power of their territory vis-à-vis other territories. The capitalist seeks individual advantage and (though usually constrained by law) is responsible to no one other than his or her immediate social circle while the statesman seeks a collective advantage and is constrained by the political and military situation of the state. The capitalist operates more in continuous (relative and relational) space and time whereas the politician is more grounded in an absolute territorial space. On the other hand, capitalist firms come and go, shift locations, merge or go out of business, but states are long-lived entities confined within fixed territorial boundaries. The dialectic of the territorial and capitalistic logics of power has far reaching effects, particularly with respect to imperialism and geopolitics.

Two distinctive but interrelated forms of geopolitical struggle (merging into imperialist practices) arise out of the capitalistic spatio-temporal logic. Imagine first a particular territory (such as an isolated state that has achieved a certain structured coherence of accumulation backed by a regional class alliance of governance). The contradictions of capital accumulation build into a crisis of overaccumulation of both capital and labor threatening massive devaluations of capital and devastating levels of unemployment. Faced with such difficulties capital seeks a "spatial fix." Capital and perhaps labor surpluses are exported elsewhere (e.g. from Britain to its colonies or to the United States in the nineteenth century). This requires, of course, that some territory be open for the penetration of capital and labor. Territories may be prized open by military force, colonization or commercial pressure, or they may voluntarily open themselves up to take advantage of surplus capitals from elsewhere (as China has done in recent years by absorbing vast amounts of foreign direct investment). The role of territorial power here is to ensure open spaces within which surplus capitals in particular can move. The effect is for capital accumulation to diffuse outwards and proliferate on the world stage. But ultimately all the territories "occupied" by capitalism will produce capital surpluses looking for a spatial fix. Geopolitical rivalries for influence or control over other territories inevitably result. This rivalry helped produce two world wars between capitalist powers in the twentieth century.

This first scenario merges into a second. Assume a more open regionality in which a variety of different interlinked territorial configurations of capital accumulation exist in different states of development. Labor and capital flows and commodity exchanges between the territories can help sustain aggregate rates of accumulation in a relatively crisis free mode provided that (a) gains from increasing territorial specialization in the division of labor are possible, (b) capital and labor surpluses in one place are matched by capital and labor shortages elsewhere, (c) barriers to movement because of high transport costs or institutional constraints (like tariffs) are systematically reduced, and (d) place specific stresses of overaccumulation do not generate a defensive posture within the regional class alliance (such as demands for protectionism). This scenario resembles, of course, several versions of interregional development proposed in bourgeois economics in which gains from trade, comparative advantages and the like can be integrated into dynamic patterns of mutually supportive economic growth. The spatial fix appears to work to the long-term stabilization of capitalism, confining crisis formation and devaluation to localized events (the closure of plants here and rising unemployment there).

This "happy and virtuous circle" of events is disrupted by two major factors. On the one hand competition between regional class alliances exercises a coercive power. Internal political structures are forced to adjust to unwelcome external pressures (the structural adjustment programs of the International Monetary Fund are of this sort). Regions are forced into some hierarchy of powers and interests such that the richer regions grow richer and the poor languish in indebtedness. Internal unrest, disruptions in the class alliance of governance and belligerence towards external powers may result. But even more important is the problem of global crises, as overaccumulation emerges everywhere as a chronic problem (the great depression of the 1930s is the classic case). The symbiotic and mutually supportive relations between territories is registered as competition over who is to bear the costs of devaluation. Geopolitical struggles then ensue at the global scale, with unpredictable outcomes and potentially violent consequences.

The politics of social struggles

Lurking within the argument of the last section is the idea that struggles between classes and class factions, though deeply embedded in the dynamics of capital accumulation, do no more than disturb or redirect the micro-dynamics of an overall system fully capable of reproducing itself albeit through the uncertain geopolitics of crisis formation and resolution. This is merely a convenient fiction and immediately poses the question as to what happens when class and factional as well as other forms of political and social struggle emerge as active determinants of uneven geographical developments. Struggles for national liberation, for the right of nations to exist as coherent state forms reflective of ethnic identities or religious affiliations, cannot be brushed aside as minor irritations in capitalism's historical geography. But by the same token I think it wrong to view such struggles as if they are entirely independent of processes of accumulation by dispossession or disconnected from the general dynamics of capital accumulation in space and time. Since capital accumulation entails territorial class alliance formation, the production of some sort of regionality and geopolitical confrontations, for example, it is highly likely that any struggles over ethnic or religious identity and autonomy will interweave and combine with all of these forces. The same connectivity will likely exist with accumulation by dispossession. This sort of interweaving is crucial for understanding something as complicated and dramatic as the longstanding Israeli-Palestinian conflict, for example. While a conflict of this sort cannot be reduced to some mix of accumulation by dispossession and expanded reproduction of capital, it cannot be viewed as having an entirely independent and autonomous existence either. It is the inner connections that are most intriguing to unravel. It is useful, therefore, to examine the varying character of social struggles in relation to the other three elements within the theoretical structure.

Social movements and accumulation by dispossession

Struggles over primitive accumulation and accumulation by dispossession are legion both in the past as well as in today's world. We should therefore pay careful attention to their provenence, their structures and their meanings. Political ethnographies and social movement studies provide abundant evidence of a vast canvas of such struggles from all around the world. These struggles are of an almost infinite variety. The most obvious tangible struggles are over access to land and living space, and to fundamental resources such as water, biomass (forests), energy and the like. The struggles over dignity, recognition, self-expression, acknowledgement of certain rights (traditional, cultural and customary) are no less salient although, by their very nature, they are much harder to pin down except by way of their effects. Movements around such issues also exhibit an almost infinite variety of objectives – some backward looking and desirous of return to some pre-existing (real or imagined) socio-ecological order, others seeking to realize more utopian and futuristic aims while still others seek pragmatic solutions to immediate problems of social or political exclusions or particular environmental degradations and injustices.

The point here is not to try to synthesize or homogenize such struggles into some general set of laws, but to unravel how so many of these on-going struggles internalize the general problematics of accumulation by dispossession. For example, the Palestinian struggle for restoration of rights to land and water is foundational for understanding the Middle East conflict and it connects with broader geopolitical struggles over the dynamics of capital accumulation within the region. The argument here is not reductionist but dialectical: while a conflict of this sort is obviously expressive of long-standing hatreds and resentments, the conditions of its amelioration inevitably entail addressing the problems that have arisen out of the dispossession of access to land and to water. Confronting these tangible questions is at the very least a necessary condition for understanding the nature of the problem and the uneven geographical developments that inform the broader regional conflict.

One cannot, I conclude, probe very far into conflicts of this kind without encountering the theme of dispossession or exclusion. Increasingly this dispossession goes far beyond the amassing of raw power of one social group versus another and has more and more to do with amassing power in relation to and through the accumulation of capital. The latter, after all, is now the prime means by which power is amassed and circulated. The pervasiveness of this general theme of accumulation by dispossession is only matched by the astonishing variety of circumstances and situations in which it is manifest. The seemingly infinite variety of struggles over what is being dispossessed, by whom, and what to do about it adds an unpredictable allure to the dynamics of capital accumulation in space and time. But the sheer unpredictability of it all in no way denies the necessity of making this aspect of political struggle a major component in any general theory of uneven geographical development.

Conflicts around the expanded reproduction of capital

If we go back over the whole dynamics of how the accumulation process works in space and time, then we immediately identify a variety of points around which social struggles of various sorts are likely to occur. The most obvious, and for Marxists the most salient locus of conflict, arises out of the class antagonism between capital and labor in surplus value production. Conflicts over wage rates, conditions of contract, living standards, conditions of the labor process, length of working day/year/life, and the like, are omnipresent and they spill over into the political arena to become a vital ingredient of what the capitalist state inevitably engages with. Struggles over skill formation and definition, divisions and fragmentations of labor (around issues of race, ethnicity and gender, for example) also enter into the picture in sometimes disruptive and violent ways. The balance of class forces and powers within any regional class alliance and its state apparatus obviously varies greatly from place to place depending upon forms of organization, levels of class consciousness, collective memories and traditions, and the like. Equally important, however, are the struggles that arise around regionality directly: the geography of infrastructural investments, territorialization of administration and collective action, class alliance formation, and struggles for geopolitical advantage. While these are omnipresent, the Marxist tradition tends to pay far more attention to the first group of direct struggles between capital and labor over surplus value production. This is unfortunate since the latter forms of struggle focus directly on uneven geographical developments, not merely as an outcome but also as an active agent powering the overall dynamics of capital accumulation. If competition between territorial units (such as states or cities) drives the capitalist dynamic ever onwards, for example, then the rise of particular regions as successful and highly competitive centers of capital accumulation affects the global situation. If the Pearl River Delta, for example, becomes one of the most dynamic and successful centers of capital accumulation through man-ufacturing in the whole world then this sets base-line standards every-where with respect to labor costs, acceptable conditions of work, technological mixes, union organizing, and the like. The deindustrialization of the rest of the world (even in low wage countries like Mexico and Brazil) occurs as the China powerhouse takes over.

The outcomes of such processes, which are so central to any theory of uneven geographical development are contingent on the nature of alliances struck within territories and the restless, shifting flows of capital, labor, information, etc. across the global space. While this is all fairly obvious in principle, it is by no means easy to track down the inner connections between struggles over the expanded reproduction of capitalism and the intricate role played by uneven geographical developments in the overall dynamics of capital accumulation. This is the issue that has, however, to be firmly and explicitly explored in any general theory of uneven geographical development.

Conflicts over the material embedding of social processes in 'the web of life'

Capitalism treats as commodities many of the fundamental elements within the web of life that are not produced as commodities. This applies to labor, to all of what we often refer to as 'nature' as well as specific forms of our social existence (most obviously money but also such features as culture, tradition, intelligence, memory, as well as the physical reproduction of the species). Once the body becomes a blatant "accumulation strategy," then alienation follows (though whether this is greeted by revolt or passive resignation is an open question). The "commodification of everything" infects every aspect of daily life. Polanyi portrayed the consequences this way:

> To allow the market mechanism to be sole director of the fate of human beings and their natural environment . . . would result in the demolition of society. For the alleged commodity 'labor power' cannot be shoved about, used indiscriminately, or even left unused, without affecting also the human individual who happens to be the bearer of this peculiar commodity. In disposing of man's labor power the system would, incidentally, dispose of the physical, psychological, and moral entity 'man' attached to that tag. Robbed of the protective covering of cultural institutions, human beings would perish from the effects of social exposure; they would die as

victims of acute social dislocation through vice, perversion, crime
and starvation. Nature would be reduced to its elements, neighborhoods and landscapes defiled, rivers polluted, military safety jeo-
pardized, the power to produce food and raw materials destroyed.
Finally, the market administration of purchasing power would
periodically liquidate business enterprise, for shortages and surfeits
of money would prove as disastrous to business as floods and
droughts in primitive society.[19]

Polanyi is here elaborating on Marx's fundamental proposition that
an unregulated free market capitalism could only survive by destroying
the two main sources of its own wealth: the land and the laborer.
Struggles consequently arise around the ways in which commodification affects the web of life. Individuals and collectivities inevitably seek
to protect themselves and others from the destructions that Polanyi
identifies. The active defense of environments, of social relations, of
processes of social reproduction, of collective memories and cultural
traditions then follows. A lot of struggles arise in this domain and many
of them are at the very minimum weakly anti-capitalistic as they seek to
re-establish those "protective coverings" that Polanyi invokes. Movements against the destructive consequences of commodification – such
as environmentalism – are not necessarily concordant with other forms
of social movement yet they are just as firmly pitted against the
dynamics of free-market capital accumulation. Everyday, material life
struggles in the socio-ecological realm are infused with meanings that
derive from commodification and its associated fetishisms. The quest
for alternatives – socialism, environmentalism, anarchism, feminism,
and the like – most conspicuously fail when they are unable to address
daily life issues in a satisfactory way.

The variety of anti-capitalist struggles we see around us, I conclude,
vary in part because of the different conditions that give rise to them.
Political struggles have a rather different character depending upon
which element is dominant in their definition. The unities within these
diverse political struggles can, however, be identified without sub-

---

19. Polanyi, *The Great Transformation*, *op. cit.*, p. 73.

merging their differences. This should make it easier to think through their interlinkages within a broad-based and global anti-capitalist movement. Plainly, not all of these struggles are "class struggles" in the classic Marxist sense. Ignoring the multi-faceted nature of such struggles under contemporary conditions is tantamount to foregoing the creation of anti-capitalist alliances that can actually do something to check if not transform what a predatory capitalism is about.

Commentary

If capitalism survives through uneven geographical development, if capitalism *is* uneven geographical development, then, surely, we need to search out an adequate theoretical framework to encompass this fact. These notes do not exhaust the field of possibilities. Theory can never provide a complete or definitive account of the world. Theory is, in any case, always something that is (or should be) in the course of formation. The elements I have here assembled are disparate, but this is precisely what makes their inclusion in the search for a pertinent theoretical framework both interesting and rich in possibilities.

I also argued that case study work should internalize theorizing practices. It remains to say something about that process. The study recently re-published as *Paris, Capital of Modernity* was for me a critical experience in this regard. I carried it out in parallel with the theoretical work on capital accumulation in space and time that was published as *The Limits to Capital*. While I had always seen the two works as moving on parallel tracks, the initial intent was to see how far the theory of capital accumulation that Marx proposed could, when properly extended to encompass spatio-temporal dynamics, explain the transformations that occurred in Paris during the Second Empire and provide a deeper understanding of the Paris Commune of 1871. The elaboration of the theory of capital accumulation in space and time was accomplished independently of the materialist enquiry. This was done by extending Marx's dialectical mode of argumentation to arenas such as fixed capital formation, investments in the built environment, finance capital, rent, spatial structures and the state. The results of that theorizing are broadly reflected in the third section of this essay. This process of theorization through abstraction generated all manner of useful insights and helped frame and re-frame many of the fundamental questions that arose in the Paris study.

But that theory, while revealing and rich in certain respects, could nowhere near exhaust the complex intertwinings of processes and forces at work in the re-shaping of Second Empire Paris. It became evident that a much broader theoretical framework was required, in which the theoretical insights already available from elaborating on Marx's theory of capital accumulation could be embedded and transformed rather than abandoned. Marx, in a way, posed that question himself by leaving dangling the question of the relation between *Capital* and his work on *Class Struggles in France* and *The Eighteenth Brumaire of Louis Bonaparte*.[20] What I have presented in these notes is, in effect, the theorizing that arose out of the Paris study as I sought to bridge the gulf between what some have erroneously dubbed "the two Marxisms" of *Capital* and *The Eighteenth Brumaire*. All of the elements I here spell out for separate scrutiny, as grist for theoretical reflection, are co-present within the Paris study. What I offer here is a set of reflections and proposals for the reformulation of theory in the light of that experience. While *The Limits to Capital* describes my theoretical framework going into the Paris study, these notes describe the framework of theorizing that came out of it.

These notes towards a unified field theory of uneven geographical development constitute, therefore, one small step, based upon a particular case study, within the on-going and endless search for a proper theoretical framing of one of the most intriguing and politically salient features of our contemporary world – its chronic and ever-fluctuating state of uneven geographical development.

20. K. Marx, *The Eighteenth Brumaire of Louis Bonaparte* (New York: International Publishers, 1963 edition); *Class Struggles in France, 1848–1850* (New York: International Publishers, 1964); D. Harvey, *Paris, Capital of Modernity* (New York: Routledge, 2003); Harvey, *Limits to Capital, op. cit.*

SPACE AS A KEYWORD

Space as a key word

David Harvey

If Raymond Williams were contemplating the entries for his celebrated text on *Keywords* today, he would surely have included the word "space." He may well have included it in that short list of concepts, such as "culture" and "nature", to be listed as "one of the most complicated words in our language."[1] How, then, can the range of meanings that attach to the word "space" be clarified without losing ourselves in some labyrinth (itself an interesting spatial metaphor) of complications?

"Space" often elicits modification. Complications sometimes arise from the modifications (which all too frequently get omitted in the telling or the writing) rather than from any inherent complexity in the notion of space itself. When, for example, we write of "material", "metaphorical", "liminal", "personal", "social" or "psychic" space (just to take a few examples) we indicate a variety of contexts that so inflect matters as to render the meaning of space contingent upon the context. Similarly, when we construct phrases such as spaces of fear, of play, of cosmology, of dreams, of anger, of particle physics, of capital, of geopolitical tension, of hope, of memory, or of ecological inter-action (again, just to indicate a few of the seemingly infinite sites of

---

1. R. Williams, *Keywords: A Vocabulary of Culture and Society* (Oxford: Oxford University Press, revised edition, 1985).

deployment of the term) then the terrain of application defines something so special as to render any generic definition of space a hopeless task. In what follows, however, I will lay aside these difficulties and attempt a general clarification of the meaning of the term. I hope thereby to disperse some of the fog of mis-communication that seems to bedevil use of the word.

The entry point we choose for such an enquiry is not innocent, however, since it inevitably defines a particular perspective that highlights some matters while occluding others. A certain privilege is, of course, usually accorded to philosophical reflection, since philosophy aspires to rise above the various and divergent fields of human practices and partial knowledges, in order to assign definitive meanings to the categories to which we may appeal. I have formed the impression that there is sufficient dissension and confusion among the philosophers as to the meaning of space as to make that anything but an unproblematic starting point. Furthermore, since I am by no means qualified to reflect on the concept of space from within the philosophical tradition, it seems best to begin at the point I know best. I therefore start from the standpoint of the geographer, not because this is a privileged site that somehow has a proprietary right (as some geographers sometimes seem to claim) over the use of spatial concepts, but because that is where I happen to do most of my work. It is in this arena that I have wrestled most directly with the complexity of what the word "space" might be all about. I have, of course, frequently drawn upon the work of others operating within various branches of the academic and intellectual division of labor as well as upon the work of many geographers (too many to be acknowledged in a brief essay of this sort) who have been actively engaged in exploring these problems in their own distinctive ways. I make no attempt here to build a synthesis of all this work. I give a purely personal account of how my own views have evolved (or not) as I have sought meanings that work, as satisfactorily as possible, for the theoretical and practical topics of primary concern to me.

I began reflecting upon this problem many years ago. In *Social Justice and the City*, published in 1973, I argued that it was crucial to reflect on the nature of space if we were to understand urban processes under capitalism. Drawing upon ideas previously culled from a study of the philosophy of science and partially explored in *Explanation in Geography*, I identified a tripartite division in the way space could be understood:

> If we regard space as absolute it becomes a 'thing in itself' with an existence independent of matter. It then possesses a structure which we can use to pigeon-hole or individuate phenomena. The view of relative space proposes that it be understood as a relationship between objects which exists only because objects exist and relate to each other. There is another sense in which space can be viewed as relative and I choose to call this relational space – space regarded in the manner of Leibniz, as being contained in objects in the sense that an object can be said to exist only insofar as it contains and represents within itself relationships to other objects.[2]

I think this tripartite division is well-worth sustaining. So let me begin with a brief elaboration on what each of these categories might entail.

Absolute space is fixed and we record or plan events within its frame. This is the space of Newton and Descartes and it is usually represented as a pre-existing and immoveable grid amenable to standardized measurement and open to calculation. Geometrically it is the space of Euclid and therefore the space of all manner of cadastral mapping and engineering practices. It is a primary space of individuation – *res extensa* as Descartes put it – and this applies to all discrete and bounded phenomena including you and me as individual persons. Socially this is the space of private property and other bounded territorial designations (such as states, administrative units, city plans and urban grids). When Descartes' engineer looked upon the world with a sense of mastery, it was a world of absolute space (and time) from which all uncertainties and ambiguities could in principle be banished and in which human calculation could uninhibitedly flourish.

The relative notion of space is mainly associated with the name of Einstein and the non-Euclidean geometries that began to be constructed most systematically in the 19th century. Space is relative in the

2. D. Harvey, *Social Justice and the City* (London: Edward Arnold, 1973) p. 13.

double sense: that there are multiple geometries from which to choose and that the spatial frame depends crucially upon what it is that is being relativized and by whom. When Gauss first established the rules of a non-Euclidean spherical geometry to deal with the problems of surveying accurately upon the curved surface of the earth, he also affirmed Euler's assertion that a perfectly scaled map of any portion of the earth's surface is impossible. Einstein took the argument further by pointing out that all forms of measurement depended upon the frame of reference of the observer. The idea of simultaneity in the physical universe, he taught us, has to be abandoned. It is impossible to understand space independent of time under this formulation and this mandates an important shift of language from space *and* time to space-time or spatio-temporality. It was, of course, Einstein's achievement to come up with exact means to examine such phenomena as the curvature of space when examining temporal processes operating at the speed of light.[3] But in Einstein's schema time remains fixed while it is space that bends according to certain observable rules (much in the same way as Gauss devised spherical geometry as an accurate means to survey through triangulation on the earth's curved surface). At the more mundane level of geographical work, we know that the space of transportation relations looks and is very different from the spaces of private property. The uniqueness of location and individuation defined by bounded territories in absolute space gives way to a multiplicity of locations that are equidistant from, say, some central city location. We can create completely different maps of relative locations by differentiating between distances measured in terms of cost, time, modal split (car, bicycle or skateboard) and even disrupt spatial continuities by looking at networks, topological relations (the optimal route for the postman delivering mail), and the like. We know, given the differential frictions of distance encountered on the earth's surface, that the shortest distance (measured in terms of time, cost, energy expended) between two points is not necessarily given by the way the legendary crow flies. Furthermore the standpoint of the observer plays a critical role. The typical New Yorker's view of the world, as the famous Steinberg

3. R. Osserman, *The Poetry of the Universe* (New York: Doubleday, 1995).

cartoon suggests, fades very fast as one thinks about the lands to the west of the Hudson River or east of Long Island. All of this relativization, it is important to note, does not necessarily reduce or eliminate the capacity for calculability or control, but it does indicate that special rules and laws are required for the particular phenomena and processes under consideration. Difficulties do arise, however, as we seek to integrate understandings from different fields into some more unified endeavor. The spatio-temporality required to represent energy flows through ecological systems accurately, for example, may not be compatible with that of financial flows through global markets. Understanding the spatio-temporal rhythms of capital accumulation requires a quite different framework to that required to understand global climate change. Such disjunctions, though extremely difficult to work across, are not necessarily a disadvantage provided we recognize them for what they are. Comparisons between different spatio-temporal frameworks can illuminate problems of political choice (do we favor the spatio-temporality of financial flows or that of the ecological processes they typically disrupt, for example).

The relational concept of space is most often associated with the name of Leibniz who, in a famous series of letters to Clarke (effectively a stand-in for Newton) objected vociferously to the absolute view of space and time so central to Newton's theories.[4] His primary objection was theological. Newton made it seem as if even God was inside of absolute space and time rather than in command of spatio-temporality. By extension, the relational view of space holds there is no such thing as space or time outside of the processes that define them. (If God makes the world then He has also chosen, out of many possibilities, to make space and time of a particular sort). Processes do not occur *in* space but define their own spatial frame. The concept of space is embedded in or internal to process. This very formulation implies that, as in the case of relative space, it is impossible to disentangle space from time. We must therefore focus on the relationality of space-time rather than of space in isolation. The relational notion of space-time implies the idea of

4. I reviewed some of this in D. Harvey, *Justice, Nature and the Geography of Difference* (Oxford: Basil Blackwell, 1996) particularly chapter 10.

internal relations; external influences get internalized in specific processes or things through time (much as my mind absorbs all manner of
external information and stimuli to yield strange patterns of thought
including dreams and fantasies as well as attempts at rational calculation). An event or a thing at a point in space cannot be understood by
appeal to what exists only at that point. It depends upon everything else
going on around it (much as all those who enter a room to discuss bring
with them a vast array of experiential data accumulated from the
world). A wide variety of disparate influences swirling over space in the
past, present and future concentrate and congeal at a certain point (e.g.
within a conference room) to define the nature of that point. Identity,
in this argument, means something quite different from the sense we
have of it from absolute space. Thus do we arrive at an extended
version of Leibniz's concept of the monad.

Measurement becomes more and more problematic the closer we
move towards a world of relational space-time. But why would it be
presumed that space-time only exists if it is measurable and quantifiable
in certain traditional ways? This leads to some interesting reflections on
the failure (perhaps better construed as limitations) of positivism and
empiricism to evolve adequate understandings of spatio-temporal
concepts beyond those that can be measured. In a way, relational
conceptions of space-time bring us to the point where mathematics,
poetry, and music converge if not merge. And that, from a scientific (as
opposed to aesthetic) viewpoint, is anathema to those of a positivist or
crudely materialist bent. On this point the Kantian compromise of
recognizing space as real but only accessible to the intuitions tries to
build a bridge between Newton and Leibniz precisely by incorporating
the concept of space within the theory of Aesthetic Judgement. But
Leibniz's return to popularity and significance not only as the guru of
cyberspace but also as a foundational thinker in relationship to more
dialectical approaches to mind-brain issues and quantum theoretical
formulations signals some sort of urge to go beyond absolute and
relative concepts and their more easily measurable qualities as well as
beyond the Kantian compromise. But the relational terrain is an
extremely challenging and difficult terrain upon which to work. There
are many thinkers who, over the years, have applied their talents to

reflecting upon the possibilities of relational thinking. Alfred North Whitehead was fascinated by the necessity of the relational view and did much to advance it.[5] Deleuze likewise made much of these ideas both in his reflections on Leibniz (with reflections on baroque architecture and the mathematics of the fold in Leibniz's work) as well as on Spinoza.[6]

But why and how would I, as a working geographer, find the relational mode of approaching space-time useful? The answer is quite simply that there are certain topics, such as the political role of collective memories in urban processes, that can only be approached in this way. I cannot box political and collective memories in some absolute space (clearly situate them on a grid or a map) nor can I understand their circulation according to the rules, however sophisticated, of relative space-time. If I ask the question: what does Tiananmen Square or "Ground Zero" *mean*, then the only way I can seek an answer is to think in relational terms. This was the problem that I confronted when writing about The Basilica of Sacre Coeur in Paris.[7] And, as I shall shortly show, it is impossible to understand Marxian political economy without engaging with relational perspectives.

So is space (space-time) absolute, relative or relational? I simply don't know whether there is an ontological answer to that question. In my own work I think of it as being all three. This was the conclusion I reached thirty years ago and I have found no particular reason (nor heard any arguments) to make me change my mind. This is what I then wrote:

> space is neither absolute, relative or relational in itself, but it can become one or all simultaneously depending on the circumstances. The problem of the proper conceptualization of space is resolved

5. J. Fitzgerald, *Alfred North Whitehead's Early Philosophy of Space and Time* (New York: Rowman and Littlefield, 1979); I tried to come to terms with Whitehead's views in Harvey, *Justice, Nature and the Geography of Difference*, *op.cit.*

6. G. Deleuze, *The Fold: Leibniz and the Baroque* (Minneapolis: Minnesota University Press, 1992).

7. D. Harvey, "Monument and Myth," *Annals of the Association of American Geographers* 69 (1979) pp. 362–81.

through human practice with respect to it. In other words, there are no philosophical answers to philosophical questions that arise over the nature of space – the answers lie in human practice. The question 'what is space?' is therefore replaced by the question 'how is it that different human practices create and make use of different conceptualizations of space?' The property relationship, for example, creates absolute spaces within which monopoly control can operate. The movement of people, goods, services, and information takes place in a relative space because it takes money, time, energy, and the like to overcome the friction of distance. Parcels of land also capture benefits because they contain relationships with other parcels . . . in the form of rent relational space comes into its own as an important aspect of human social practice.[8]

Are there rules for deciding when and where one spatial frame is preferable to another? Or is the choice arbitrary, subject to the whims of human practice? The decision to use one or other conception certainly depends on the nature of the phenomena under investigation. The absolute conception may be perfectly adequate for issues of property boundaries and border determinations but it helps me not a whit with the question of what is Tiananmen Square, Ground Zero or the Basilica of Sacre Coeur. I therefore find it helpful – if only as an internal check – to sketch in justifications for the choice of an absolute, relative, or relational frame of reference. Furthermore, I often find myself presuming in my practices that there is some hierarchy at work among them in the sense that relational space can embrace the relative and the absolute, relative space can embrace the absolute, but absolute space is just absolute and that is that. But I would not confidently advance this view as a working principle let alone try to defend it theoretically. I find it far more interesting in principle to keep the three concepts in dialectical tension with each other and to constantly think through the interplay among them. Ground Zero is an absolute space at the same time as it is relative and relational in space-time.

Let me try to put this in a more immediate context. I give a talk in a

8. Harvey, *Social Justice and the City, op. cit.*, p. 13.

room. The reach of my words is bounded by the absolute space of those particular walls and limited to the absolute time of the talk. To hear me people have to be there within that absolute space during that absolute time. People who cannot get in are excluded and those that come later will not hear me. Those who are there can be identified as individuals – individuated – each according to the absolute space, such as the seat occupied, for that time. But I am also in a relative space with respect to my audience. I am here and they are there. I try to communicate across the space through a medium – the atmosphere – that refracts my words differentially. I talk softly and the clarity of my words fades across space: the back row can't hear at all. If there is a video-feed to Aberdeen I can be heard there but not in the back row. My words are received differentially in relative space-time. Individuation is more problematic since there are many people in exactly the same relative location to me in that space-time. All the people in the fourth row are equidistant from me. A discontinuity in space-time arises between those who can hear and those who cannot. The analysis of what is going on in the absolute space and time of the talk given in the room looks very different when analysed through the lens of relative space-time. But then there is the relational component too. Individuals in the audience bring to the absolute space and time of the talk all sorts of ideas and experiences culled from the space-time of their life trajectories and all of that is co-present in the room: he cannot stop thinking of the argument over breakfast, she cannot erase from her mind the awful images of death and destruction on last night's news. Something about the way I talk reminds someone else of a traumatic event lost in some distant past and my words remind someone else of political meetings they used to go to in the 1970s. My words express a certain fury about what is going on in the world. I find myself thinking while talking that everything we are doing in this room is stupid and trivial. There is a palpable sense of tension in the room. Why aren't we out there bringing the government down? I extricate myself from all these relationalities, retire back into the absolute and relative spaces of the room and try to address the topic of space as a key word in a dry and technical manner. The tension dissipates and someone in the front row nods off. I know where everyone is in absolute space and time but I have no idea, as the saying goes, "where peoples' heads are at." I may sense that some people are with me and some are not but I never know for sure. Yet this is, surely the most important element of all. That, after all, is where shifting political subjectivities lie. The relationality is elusive if not impossible to pin down, but it is none the less vitally important for all that.

There is, I mean to show by this example, bound to be a liminality about spatiality itself because we are inexorably situated in all three frameworks simultaneously, though not necessarily equally so. We may end up, often without noticing it, favoring one or other definition through our practical actions. In an absolutist mode, I will do one thing and reach one set of conclusions; in a relative mode, I'll construct my interpretations differently and do something else; and if everything looks different through relational filters then I will conduct myself in a quite different way. What we do as well as what we understand is integrally dependent upon the primary spatio-temporal frame within which we situate ourselves. Consider how this works in relation to that most fraught of socio-political concepts we call "identity." Everything is clear enough in absolute space and time, but things get a bit more awkward when it comes to relative space-time and downright difficult in a relational world. But it is only in this last frame that we can start to grapple with many aspects of contemporary politics since that is the world of political subjectivity and political consciousness. Du Bois long ago attempted to address this in terms of what he called "double consciousness" – what does it mean, he asked, to carry within oneself the experience of being both black and American? We now complicate the question further by asking what does it mean to be American, black, female, lesbian and working class? How do all those relationalities enter into the political consciousness of the subject? And when we consider other dimensions – of migrants, diasporic groups, tourists and travellers and those that watch the contemporary global media and partially filter or absorb its cacophony of messages – then the primary question we are faced with is understanding how this whole relational world of experience and information gets *internalized* within the particular political subject (albeit individuated in absolute space and time) to support this or that line of thinking and of action. Plainly, we cannot understand the shifting terrain upon which political subjectivities are formed and political actions occur without thinking about what happens in relational terms.

If the contrast between absolute, relative and relational conceptions of space is the only way to unpack the meaning of space as a key word, then matters could safely be left here. Fortunately or unfortunately, there are other and equally cogent ways to address the problem. Many geographers in recent years, for example, have pointed to a key difference in the deployment of the concept of space as an essential element in a materialist project of understanding tangible geographies on the ground and the widespread appropriation of spatial metaphors within social, literary and cultural theory. These metaphors, furthermore, have frequently been used to disrupt so-called metanarratives (such as Marxian theory) and those discursive strategies in which the temporal dimension typically prevails. All of this has provoked an immense debate on the role of space in social, literary and cultural theory. I do not intend to get into any detailed discussion of the significance of this so-called "spatial turn" in general and its relation to postmodernism in particular. But my own position has been fairly clear throughout: of course the proper consideration of space and space-time has crucial effects upon how theories and understandings get articulated and developed. But this creates absolutely no justification whatsoever for turning away from all attempts at any kind of metatheory (the end result would be to take us back to geography as it was practiced in the academy in the 1950s, which is, interestingly where a significant segment of contemporary British Geography seems to be happily, if unwittingly, substantively headed). The point about grappling with space as a key word is therefore to identify how this concept might be better integrated into existing social, literary and cultural metatheories and with what effects.

Cassirer, for example, sets up a tripartite division of modes of human spatial experience, distinguishing between *organic, perceptual* and *symbolic* spaces.[9] Under the first he arranges all those forms of spatial

9. E. Cassirer, *An Essay on Man* (New Haven: Yale University Press, 1944); see also Harvey, *Social Justice and the City, op. cit.*, p. 28.

experience given biologically (hence materially and registered through the particular characteristics of our senses). Perceptual space refers to the ways we process the physical and biological experience of space neurologically and register it in the world of thought. Symbolic space, on the other hand, is abstract (and may entail the development of an abstract symbolic language like geometry or the construction of architectural or pictorial forms). Symbolic space generates distinctive meanings through readings and interpretations. The question of aesthetic practices here comes to the fore. In this domain, Langer, for her part, distinguishes between "real" and "virtual space." The latter, in her view, amounts to a "created space built out of forms, colours, and so on" so as to produce the intangible images and illusions that constitute the heart of all aesthetic practices. Architecture, she argues, "is a plastic art, and its first achievement is always, unconsciously and inevitably, an illusion: something purely imaginary or conceptual translated into visual impression." What exists in the real space can be described easily enough but in order to understand the affect that comes with exposure to the work of art we have to explore the very different world of virtual space. And this, she holds, always projects us into a distinctively ethnic domain.[10] These were the sorts of ideas I first encountered in *Social Justice and the City*.

It is out of this tradition of spatialized thought that Lefebvre (almost certainly drawing upon Cassirer) constructs his own distinctive tripartite division of material space (the space of experience and of perception open to physical touch and sensation); the representation of space (space as conceived and represented); and spaces of representation (the lived space of sensations, the imagination, emotions, and meanings incorporated into how we live day by day).[11]

If I focus on Lefebvre here it is not because, as so many in cultural and literary theory seem to suppose, that Lefebvre provides the originary moment from which all thinking about the production of space derives (such a thesis is manifestly absurd), but because I find it

---

10. S. Langer, *Feeling and Form: A Theory of Art* (New York: Prentice Hall, 1953); see also Harvey, Social Justice and the City *op. cit.*, p. 31.
11. H. Lefebvre, *The Production of Space* (Oxford: Basil Blackwell, 1991).

more convenient to work with Lefebvre's categories rather than Cassirer's. Material space is, for us humans, quite simply the world of tactile and sensual interaction with matter, it is the space of experience. The elements, moments and events in that world are constituted out of a materiality of certain qualities. How we represent this world is an entirely different matter, but here too we do not conceive of or represent space in arbitrary ways, but seek some appropriate if not accurate reflection of the material realities that surround us through abstract representations (words, graphs, maps, diagrams, pictures, etc.). But Lefebvre, like Benjamin, insists that we do not live as material atoms floating around in a materialist world; we also have imaginations, fears, emotions, psychologies, fantasies and dreams.[12] These spaces of representation are part and parcel of the way we live in the world. We may also seek to represent the way this space is emotively and affectively as well as materially lived by means of poetic images, photographic compositions, artistic reconstructions. The strange spatio-temporality of a dream, a fantasy, a hidden longing, a lost memory or even a peculiar thrill or tingle of fear as we walk down a street can be given representation through works of art that ultimately always have a mundane presence in absolute space and time. Leibniz, too, had found the whole question of alternate spatio-temporal worlds and dreams of considerable interest.

It is tempting, as with the first tripartite division of spatial terms we considered, to treat of Lefebvre's three categories as hierarchically ordered, but here too it seems most appropriate to keep the three categories in dialectical tension. The physical and material experience of spatial and temporal ordering is mediated to some degree by the way space and time are represented. The oceanographer/physicist swimming among the waves may experience them differently from the poet enamored of Walt Whitman or the pianist who loves Debussy. Reading a book about Patagonia will likely affect how we experience that place when we travel there even if we experience considerable cognitive dissonance between expectations generated by the written word and how it actually feels upon the ground. The spaces and times

12. W. Benjamin, *The Arcades Project* (Cambridge, Mass.: Belknap Press, 1999).

of representation that envelop and surround us as we go about our daily lives likewise affect both our direct experiences and the way we interpret and understand representations. We may not even notice the material qualities of spatial orderings incorporated into daily life because we adhere to unexamined routines. Yet it is through those daily material routines that we absorb a certain sense of how spatial representations work and build up certain spaces of representation for ourselves (e.g. the visceral sense of security in a familiar neighborhood or of being "at home"). We only notice when something appears radically out of place. It is, I want to suggest, the dialectical relation between the categories that really counts, even though it is useful for purposes of understanding to crystallize each element out as distinctive moments to the experience of space and time.

This mode of thinking about space helps me interpret works of art and architecture. A picture, like Munch's *The Scream*, is a material object but it works from the standpoint of a psychic state (Lefebvre's space of representation or lived space), and attempts through a particular set of representational codes (the representation of space or conceived space) to take on a physical form (the material space of the picture open to our actual physical experience) that says something to us about the qualities of how Munch lived that space. He seems to have had some sort of horrific nightmare, the sort from which we wake up screaming. And he has managed to convey something of the sense of that through the physical object. Many contemporary artists, making use of multimedia and kinetic techniques, create experiential spaces in which several modes of experiencing space-time combine. Here, for example, is how Judith Barry's contribution to the Third Berlin Biennial for Contemporary Art is described in the catalogue:

> In her experimental works, video artist Judith Barry investigates the use, construction and complex interaction of private and public spaces, media, society, and genders. The themes of her installations and theoretical writings position themselves in a field of observation that addresses historical memory, mass communication, and percep-tion. In a realm between the viewer's imagination and media-generated architecture, she creates imaginary spaces, alienated de-

pictions of profane reality . . . In the work *Voice Off*. . . the viewer penetrates the claustrophobic crampedness of the exhibition space, goes deeper into the work, and, forced to move through the installation, experiences not only cinematic but also cinemaesthetic impressions. The divided projection space offers the possibility of making contact with different voices. The use and hearing of voices as a driving force, and the intensity of the psychic tension – especially on the male side of the projection, – conveys the inherent strength of this intangible and ephemeral object. The voices demonstrate for spectators how one can change through them, how one tries to take control of them and the loss one feels when they are no longer heard.

Barry, the catalogue concludes, "stages aesthetic spaces of transit that leave the ambivalence between seduction and reflection unresolved."[13]

But to grapple fully with this description of Barry's work, we need to take the concepts of space and space-time to a deeper level of complexity. There is much in this description that escapes the Lefebvrian categories but refers back to the distinctions between absolute space and time (the cramped physical structure of the exhibit), relative space-time (the sequential motion of the visitor through the space) and relational space time (the memories, the voices, the psychic tension, the intangibility and ephemerality, as well as the claustrophobia). Yet we cannot let go of the Lefebvrian categories either. The constructed spaces have material, conceptual and lived dimensions.

I propose, therefore, a speculative leap in which we place the threefold division of absolute, relative and relational space-time up against the tripartite division of experienced, conceptualized and lived space identified by Lefebvre. The result is a three-by-three matrix within which points of intersection suggest different modalities of understanding the meanings of space and space-time. It may properly be objected that I am here restricting possibilities because a matrix mode of representation is self-confined to an absolute space. This is a perfectly valid objection. And insofar as I am here engaging in a

13. Third Berlin Biennial for Contemporary Art, *Catalogue: Judith Barry, Voice Off* (Berlin: Biennale, 2004) pp. 48–9.

representational practice (conceptualization) I cannot do justice to either the experienced or the lived realms of spatiality either. By definition, therefore, the matrix I set up and the way I can use it has limited revelatory power. But with all that conceded, I find it helpful to consider the combinations that arise at different intersections within the matrix. The virtue of representation in absolute space is that it allows us to individuate phenomena with great clarity. And with a bit of imagination it is possible to think dialectically across the elements within the matrix so that each moment is imagined as an internal relation of all the others. I illustrate the sort of thing I have in mind (in a somewhat condensed, arbitrary and schematic form) in Figure 1. The entries within the matrix are merely suggestive rather than definitive (readers might enjoy constructing their own entries just to get some sense of my meaning).

I find it helpful to read across or down the matrix of categories and to imagine complex scenarios of combination. Imagine, for example, the absolute space of an affluent gated community on the New Jersey shore. Some of the inhabitants move in relative space on a daily basis into and out of the financial district of Manhattan where they set in motion movements of credit and investment moneys that affect social life across the globe, earning thereby the immense money power that permits them to import back into the absolute space of their gated community all of the energy, exotic foods and wondrous commodities they need to secure their privileged lifestyle. The inhabitants feel vaguely threatened, however, because they sense that there is a visceral, undefinable and unlocatable hatred for all things American arising in the world out there and its name is "terrorism." They support a government that promises to protect them from this nebulous threat. But they become increasingly paranoid about the hostility they sense in the world around them and increasingly look to build up their absolute space to protect themselves, building higher and higher walls, even hiring armed guards to protect the borders. Meanwhile, their profligate consumption of energy to power their bullet-proof humvees that take them into the city every day, proves the straw that breaks the back of global climate change. Atmospheric patterns of circulation shift dramatically. Then, in the compelling but rather inaccurate popular-

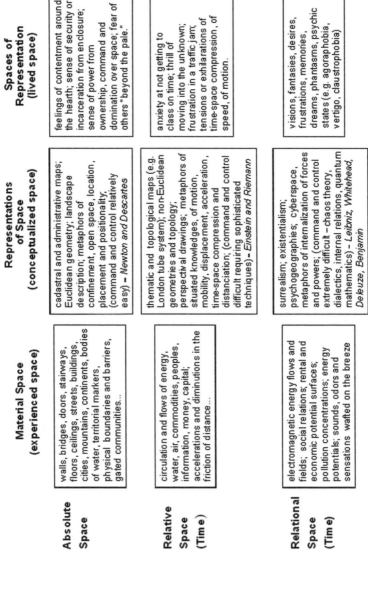

	Material Space (experienced space)	Representations of Space (conceptualized space)	Spaces of Representation (lived space)
Absolute Space	walls, bridges, doors, stairways, floors, ceilings, streets, buildings, cities, mountains, continents, bodies of water, territorial markers, physical boundaries and barriers, gated communities...	cadastral and administrative maps; Euclidean geometry; landscape description; metaphors of confinement, open space, location, placement and positionality; (command and control relatively easy) – *Newton and Descartes*	feelings of contentment around the hearth; sense of security or incarceration from enclosure; sense of power from ownership, command and domination over space; fear of others "beyond the pale."
Relative Space (Time)	circulation and flows of energy, water, air, commodities, peoples, information, money, capital; accelerations and diminutions in the friction of distance...	thematic and topological maps (e.g. London tube system); non-Euclidean geometries and topology; perspectival drawings; metaphors of situated knowledges, of motion, mobility, displacement, acceleration, time-space compression and distanciation; (command and control difficult requiring sophisticated techniques) – *Einstein and Riemann*	anxiety at not getting to class on time; thrill of moving into the unknown; frustration in a traffic jam; tensions or exhilarations of time-space compression, of speed, of motion.
Relational Space (Time)	electromagnetic energy flows and fields; social relations; rental and economic potential surfaces; pollution concentrations; energy potentials; sounds, odors and sensations wafted on the breeze	surrealism; existentialism; psychogeographies; cyberspace, metaphors of internalization of forces and powers; (command and control extremely difficult – chaos theory, dialectics, internal relations, quantum mathematics) – *Leibniz, Whitehead, Deleuze, Benjamin*	visions, fantasies, desires, frustrations, memories, dreams, phantasms, psychic states (e.g. agoraphobia, vertigo, claustrophobia)

Figure 1 A general matrix of spatialities

ized depiction of chaos theory, a butterfly flaps its wings in Hong Kong and a devastating hurricane hits the New Jersey shore and wipes out the gated community. Many residents die because they are so fearful of the outside that they ignore the warnings to evacuate. If this were a Hollywood production, a lone scientist would recognize the danger and rescue the woman he adores but who has hitherto ignored him but she now falls gratefully in love with him . . .

In the telling of a simple story of this sort it proves impossible to confine oneself to just one modality of spatial and spatio-temporal thinking. The actions taken in the absolute space only make sense in relational terms. Even more interesting, therefore, is the situation in which moments in the matrix are in more explicit dialectical tension. Let me illustrate.

What spatial and spatio-temporal principles should be deployed in re-designing the site known as "Ground Zero" in Manhattan? It is an absolute space that can be materially reconstructed and to this end engineering calculations (informed by Newtonian mechanics) and architectural designs must be made. There is much discussion about retaining walls and the load-bearing capacities of the site. Aesthetic judgments on how the space, once turned into a material artifact of some sort, might be lived as well as conceptualized and experienced also become important (Kant would approve). The problem is to so arrange the physical space as to produce an emotive effect while matching certain expectations (commercial as well as emotive and aesthetic) as to how the space might be lived. Once constructed the experience of the space may be mediated by representational forms (such as guide books and plans) that help us interpret the intended meanings of the reconstructed site. But moving dialectically across the dimension of absolute space alone is much less rewarding than the insights that come from appealing to the other spatio-temporal frames. Capitalist developers are keenly aware of the relative location of the site and judge its prospects for commercial development according to a logic of exchange relations. Its centrality and proximity to the command and control functions of Wall Street are important attributes and if transportation access can be improved in the course of reconstruction then so much the better since this can only add to land and property values. For the developers the site does not merely exist *in* relative space-time: the re-engineering of the site offers the prospect of transforming relative space-time so as to enhance the commercial value of the absolute spaces (by improving access to airports for example). The temporal horizon would be dominated by considerations of the amortization rate and the interest/discount rate applying to fixed capital investments in the built environment.

But there would almost certainly be popular objections, led by the families of those killed at that site, to thinking and building only in these absolute or relative spatio-temporal terms. Whatever is built at this site has to say something about history and memory. There will likely also be pressures to say something about the meanings of community and nation as well as about future possibilities (perhaps even a prospect of eternal truths). Nor could the site ignore the issue of relational spatial connectivity to the rest of the world. Even capitalist developers would not be averse to combining their mundane commercial concerns with inspiring symbolic statements (emphasizing the power and indestructibility of the political-economic system of global capitalism that received such a body blow on 9/11) by erecting, say, a towering phallic symbol that spells defiance. They, too, seek expressive power in relational space-time. But there are all manner of relationalities to be explored. What will we know about those who attacked and how far will we connect? The site is and will have a relational presence in the world no matter what is built there and it is important to reflect on how this presencing works: will it be lived as a symbol of US arrogance or as a sign of global compassion and understanding? Taking up such matters requires that we embrace a relational conception of space-time.

If, as Benjamin has it, history (a relative temporal concept) is not the same as memory (a relational temporal concept) then we have a choice of whether to historicize the events of 9/11 or to seek to memorialize them. If the site is merely historicized in relative space (by a certain sort of monumentality) then this imposes a fixed narrative on the space. The effect will be to foreclose on future possibilities and interpretations. Such closure will tend to constrict the generative power to build a different future. Memory, on the other hand, is, according to Benjamin, a potentiality that can at times "flash up" uncontrollably at times of crisis to reveal new possibilities.[14] The way the site might be lived by those who encounter it then becomes unpredictable and uncertain. Collective memory, a diffuse but nevertheless powerful sense that pervades many an urban scene, can play a significant role in animating political and social movements. Ground Zero cannot be anything other than a site of collective memory and the problem for the designers is to translate that diffuse sensibility into the absolute spaces of bricks, mortar, steel and glass. And if, as Balzac once put it, "hope is a memory that desires" then the creation of a "space of hope" on that spot requires that memory be internalized there at the same time as ways are left open for the expression of desire.[15]

The expressive relationality of Ground Zero in itself poses fascinating questions. The forces that converged over space to produce 9/11 were complex. How, then, can some accounting be given of these forces? Can something experienced as a local and personal tragedy be reconciled with an understanding of the international forces that were so powerfully condensed within those few shattering moments in a particular place? Will we get to feel in that space the widespread resentment in the rest of the world towards the way US hegemony was so selfishly being exercised throughout during the 1980s and 1990s? Will we get to know that the Reagan administration played a key role in creating and supporting the Taliban in Afghanistan in order to undermine the Soviet occupation and that Osama bin Laden turned from being an ally of the US into an enemy because of US support for the corrupt regime in Saudi Arabia? Or will we only learn of cowardly, alien and evil "others" out there who hated the US and sought to destroy it because of all it stood for in terms of the values of liberty and freedom? The relational spatio-temporality of the event and the site can be exhumed with enough dedicated digging. But the manner of its representation and of its materialization is uncertain. The outcome will clearly depend upon political struggle. And the fiercest battles will have to be fought over what relational space-time the rebuilding will invoke. These were the sorts of issues I encountered when I attempted to

14. W. Benjamin, *Illuminations* (New York: Schocken, 1968).
15. See D. Harvey, *Paris: Capital of Modernity* (New York: Routledge, 2003), chapter 1.

interpret the meaning of the Basilica of Sacre-Coeur in Paris against the background of the historical memory of the Paris Commune.

This brings me to some observations on the politics of the argument. Thinking through the different ways in which space and space-time get used as a key word helps define certain conditions of possibility for critical engagement. It also opens up ways to identify conflicting claims and alternative political possibilities. It invites us to consider the ways we physically shape our environment and the ways in which we both represent and get to live in it. I think it fair to say that the Marxist tradition has not been deeply engaged upon such issues and that this general failure (although there are, of course, numerous exceptions) has more often than not meant a loss of possibilities for certain kinds of transformative politics. If, for example, socialist realist art fails to capture the imagination and if the monumentality achieved under past communist regimes was so lacking in inspiration, if planned communities and communist cities often seem so dead to the world, then one way to engage critically with this problem would be to look at the modes of thinking about space and space-time and the unnecessarily limiting and constricting roles they may have played in socialist planning practices.

There has not been much explicit debate about such issues within the Marxist tradition. Yet Marx himself is a relational thinker. In revolutionary situations such as that of 1848 Marx worried that the past might weigh like a nightmare on the brain of the living and forthrightly posed the question as to how a revolutionary poetry of the future might be constructed then and there.[16] At that time he also pled with Cabet not to take his communist-minded followers to the new world. There, Marx averred, the Icarians would only re-plant the attitudes and beliefs internalized from out of the experience of the old. They should, Marx advised, stay as good communists in Europe and fight through the revolutionary transformation in that space, even though there was always the danger that a revolution made in "our little corner of the world" would fall victim to the global forces ranged around it.[17]

16. K. Marx, *The Eighteenth Brumaire of Louis Bonaparte* (New York: International Publishers, 1963).

17. Cited in L. Marin, *Utopics: A Spatial Play* (Atlantic Heights, N.J.: Humanities Press, 1984).

Lenin, plainly distressed at Mach's idealist mode of presentation, sought to reinforce the absolute and mechanistic views on space and time associated with Newton as the only proper materialist basis for scientific enquiry. He did so at the very time when Einstein was bringing relative, but equally materialist views of space-time into prominence. Lenin's strict line was to some degree softened by Lukacs's turn to a more pliable view of history and temporality. But Lukacs's constructivist views on the relation to nature were roundly rejected by Wittfogel's assertion of a hard-headed materialism that morphed into environmental determinism. In the works of Thompson, Williams and others, on the other hand, we find different levels of appreciation, particularly of the temporal dimension though space and place are also omnipresent. In Williams' novel *People of the Black Mountains* the relationality of space-time is central. Williams uses it to bind the narrative together and directly emphasizes the different ways of knowing that come with different senses of space-time:

> If lives and places were being seriously sought, a powerful attach-ment to lives and to places was entirely demanded. The polystyrene model and its textual and theoretical equivalents remained different from the substance they reconstructed and simulated . . . At his books and maps in the library, or in the house in the valley, there was a common history which could be translated anywhere, in a community of evidence and rational enquiry. Yet he had only to move on the mountains for a different kind of mind to assert itself; stubbornly native and local, yet reaching beyond to a wider common flow, where touch and breadth replaced record and analysis; not history as narrative but stories as lives.[18]

For Williams the relationality comes alive walking on the moun-tains. It centers a completely different sensibility and feeling than that constructed from the archive. Interestingly, it is only in his novels that Williams seems able to get at this problem. Within the Marxian tradition, with the exception of Lefebvre and the geographers, an

---

18. R. Williams, *People of the Black Mountains: The Beginnings* (London: Chatto and Windus, 1989) pp. 10–12.

expansive understanding of the problematics of space and time is missing. So how then can these perspectives on space and space-time become more closely integrated into our reading, interpretation, and use of Marxian theory? Let me lay aside all concern for caveats and nuances in order to present an argument in the starkest possible terms.

In the first chapter of *Capital*, Marx introduces three key concepts of use value, exchange value and value. Everything that pertains to use value lies in the province of absolute space and time (Figure 2). Individual workers, machines, commodities, factories, roads, houses and actual labor processes, expenditures of energy, and the like can all be individuated, described and understood within the Newtonian frame of absolute space and time. Everything that pertains to exchange value lies in relative space-time because exchange entails movements of commodities, money, capital, labor power and people over time and space. It is the circulation, the perpetual motion, that counts. Exchange, as Marx observes, therefore breaks through all barriers of space and time.[19] It perpetually reshapes the coordinates within which we live our daily lives. With the advent of money this "breaking through" defines an even grander and more fluid universe of exchange relations across the relative space-time of the world market (understood not as a thing but as continuous movement and interaction). The circulation and accumulation of capital occurs in relative space-time. Value is, however, a relational concept. Its referent is, therefore, relational space-time. Value, Marx states (somewhat surprisingly), is immaterial but objective. "Not an atom of matter enters into the objectivity of commodities of values." As a consequence, value does not "stalk about with a label describing what it is" but hides its relationality within the fetishism of commodities.[20] The only way we can approach it is via that peculiar world in which material relations are established between people (we relate to each other via what we produce and trade) and social relations are constructed between things (prices are set for what we produce and trade). Value is, in short, a social relation. As such, it is impossible to measure except by way of its effects (try measuring any

19. K. Marx, *Capital Vol 1* (New York: Viking Press, 1976) p. 209.
20. Ibid., p. 138; p. 167.

social relation directly and you always fail). Value internalizes the whole historical geography of innumerable labor processes set up under conditions of or in relation to capital accumulation in the space-time of the world market. Many are surprised to find that Marx's most fundamental concept is "immaterial but objective" given the way he is usually depicted as a materialist for whom anything immaterial would be anathema. This relational definition of value, I note in passing, renders moot if not misplaced all those attempts to come up with some direct and essentialist measure of it. Social relations can only ever be measured by their effects.

If my characterization of the Marxian categories is correct, then this shows no priority can be accorded to any one spatio-temporal frame. The three spatio-temporal frames must be kept in dialectical tension with each other in exactly the same way that use value, exchange value and value dialectically intertwine within the Marxian theory. There would, for example, be no value in relational space-time without concrete labors constructed in innumerable places in absolute spaces and times. Nor would value emerge as an immaterial but objective power without the innumerable acts of exchange, the continuous circulation processes, that weld together the global market in relative space-time. Value is, then a social relation that internalizes the whole history and geography of concrete labors in the world market. It is expressive of the social (primarily but not exclusively class) relations of capitalism constructed on the world stage. It is crucial to mark the temporality involved, not only because of the significance of past "dead" labor (fixed capital including all of that embedded in built environments) but also because of all the traces of the history of proletarianization, of primitive accumulation, of technological developments that are internalized within the value form. Above all, we have to acknowledge the "historical and moral elements" that always enter into the determination of the value of labor power.[21] We then see Marx's theory working in a particular way. The spinner embeds value (i.e. abstract labor as a relational determination) in the cloth by performing concrete labor in absolute space and time.

21. Ibid., p. 275.

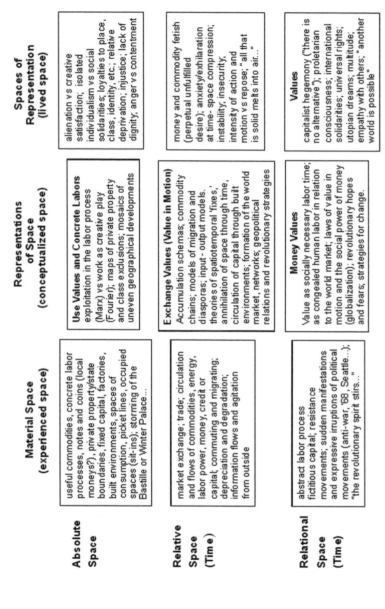

	Material Space (experienced space)	Representations of Space (conceptualized space)	Spaces of Representation (lived space)
Absolute Space	useful commodities, concrete labor processes, notes and coins (local moneys?), private property/state boundaries, fixed capital, factories, built environments, spaces of consumption, picket lines, occupied spaces (sit-ins); storming of the Bastille or Winter Palace...	**Use Values and Concrete Labors** exploitation in the labor process (Marx) vs work as creative play (Fourier); maps of private property and class exclusions; mosaics of uneven geographical developments	alienation vs creative satisfaction; isolated individualism vs social solidarities; loyalties to place, class, identity, etc.; relative deprivation; injustice; lack of dignity, anger vs contentment
Relative Space (Time)	market exchange; trade; circulation and flows of commodities, energy, labor power, money, credit or capital; commuting and migrating; depreciation and degradation; information flows and agitation from outside	**Exchange Values (Value in Motion)** Accumulation schemas; commodity chains; models of migration and diasporas; input-output models. theories of spatiotemporal 'fixes,' annihilation of space through time, circulation of capital through built environments; formation of the world market, networks; geopolitical relations and revolutionary strategies	money and commodity fetish (perpetual unfulfilled desire); anxiety/exhilaration at time-space compression; instability; insecurity; intensity of action and motion vs repose, "all that is solid melts into air..."
Relational Space (Time)	abstract labor process fictitious capital; resistance movements; sudden manifestations and expressive irruptions of political movements (anti-war, '68, Seattle...); "the revolutionary spirit stirs..."	**Money Values** Value as socially necessary labor time; as congealed human labor in relation to the world market; laws of value in motion and the social power of money (globalization); revolutionary hopes and fears, strategies for change.	**Values** capitalist hegemony ("there is no alternative"); proletarian consciousness; international solidarities; universal rights; utopian dreams; multitude; empathy with others; "another world is possible"

Figure 2 A matrix of spatialities for Marxian theory

The objective power of the value relation is registered when the spinner is forced to give up making the cloth and the factory falls silent because conditions in the world market are such as to make this activity in that particular absolute space and time valueless. While all of this may seem obvious, the failure to acknowledge the interplay entailed between the different spatio-temporal frames in Marxian theory often produces conceptual confusion. Much discussion of so-called "global-local relations" has become a conceptual muddle, for example, because of the inability to understand the different spatio-temporalities involved. We cannot say that the value relation causes the factory to close down as if it is some external abstract force. It is the changing concrete conditions of labor in China when mediated through exchange processes in relative space time that transforms value as a social relation in such a way as to bring the concrete labor process in Mexico to closure.

So far, I have largely confined attention to a dialectical reading of Marxian theory down the left hand column of the matrix. What happens when I start to read across the matrix instead? The materiality of use values and concrete labors is obvious enough. But how can this be represented and conceived? Physical descriptions are easy to produce but Marx insists that the social relations under which work is performed are critical also. Under capitalism the wage laborer is conceptualized (second column) as a producer of surplus value for the capitalist and this is represented as a relation of exploitation. This implies that the labor process is lived (third column) as alienation. Under different social relations, e.g. those of socialism, work could be lived as creative satisfaction and conceptualized as self-realization through collective endeavors. It may not even have to change materially in order for it to be reconceptualized and lived in a quite different way. This was, after all, Lenin's hope when he advocated the adoption of Fordism in Soviet factories. Fourier, for his part, thought that work should be about play and the expression of desire and be lived as sublime joy and for that to happen the material qualities of work processes would need to be radically restructured. At this point we have to acknowledge a variety of competing possibilities. In his book *Manufacturing Consent,* for example, Burawoy found that the workers in the factory he studied did not generally experience work as alienation.[22] This arose because they smothered the idea of exploitation by turning the workplace into a site for role and game-playing (Fourier style). The labor process was performed by the workers in such a way as to permit them to live the process in a non-alienated way. There are some advantages for capital in this, since unalienated workers often work more efficiently. Capitalists have therefore acceded to various measures, such as calisthenics, quality circles, and the like, to try to reduce alienation and to emphasize incorporation. They have also produced alternative conceptualizations that emphasize the rewards of hard work and produce ideologies to negate the theory of exploitation. While the Marxian theory of exploitation may be formally correct, therefore, it does not always or necessarily translate into alienation and political resistance. Much depends on how it is conceptualized. The consequences for political consciousness and working class action are wide-ranging. Part of class struggle is therefore about driving home the significance of exploitation as the proper conceptualization of how concrete labors are accomplished under capitalist social relations. Again, it is the dialectical tension between the material, the conceived and the lived that really matters. If we treat the tensions in a mechanical way then we are lost.

While working through matters in this way is helpful, I earlier argued that the "matrix thinking" offers limited opportunities unless we are prepared to range freely and dialectically over all the moments of the matrix simultaneously. Let me give an example. The primary form of representation of value is through money. This too is an immaterial concept with objective power but it must also take on material form as an actual use value. This it does in the first instance through the emergence of the money commodity (e.g. gold). The emergence occurs, however, through acts of exchange in relative space-time and it is this that allows tangible money forms to become an active presence in absolute space and time. This creates the paradox that a particular material use value (such as gold or a dollar bill) has to represent the universality of value, of abstract

22. M. Burawoy, *Manufacturing Consent: Changes in the Labor Process Under Monopoly Capitalism* (Chicago: Chicago University Press, 1982).

labor. It further implies that social power can be appropriated by private persons and from this the very possibility of money as capital placed in circulation in relative space-time arises. There are, as Marx points out, many antinomies, antitheses and contradictions in how money is created, conceptualized, circulated, and used as both a tangible means of circulation and a representation of value on the world market. Precisely because value is immaterial and objective, money always combines fictitious qualities with tangible forms. It is subject to that reversal Marx describes in the fetishism of commodities such that material relations arise between people and social relations are registered between things. Money as an object of desire and as an object of neurotic contemplation imprisons us in fetishisms while the inherent contradictions in the money form inevitably produce not only the possibility but also the inevitability of capitalist crises. Money anxieties are frequently with us and have their own spatio-temporal locations (the impoverished child that pauses before the vast panoply of capitalist commodities perpetually beyond reach in the window of the store). The spectacles of consumption that litter the landscape in absolute space and time can generate senses of relative deprivation. We are surrounded at every turn with manifestations of the fetish desire for money power as the representation of value on the world market.

For those unfamiliar with Marxian theory, this will all doubtless appear rather mysterious. The point, however, is to illustrate how theoretical work (and I would like to suggest this should be true of all social, literary and cultural theory) invariably and necessarily entails at the very minimum moving dialectically across all points within the matrix and then beyond. The more we move the greater the depth and range of our understandings. There are no discrete and closed boxes in this system. The dialectical tensions must not only be kept intact. They must be continuously expanded.

I end, however, with some cautionary remarks. In recent years many academics, including geographers, have embraced relational concepts and ways of thinking (though not very explicitly with respect to those of space-time). This move, as crucial as it is laudable, has to some degree been associated with the cultural and postmodern turn. But in the same way that traditional and positivist geography limited its vision by concentrating exclusively on the absolute and relative and upon the material and conceptual aspects of space-time (eschewing the lived and the relational), so there is a serious danger of dwelling only upon the relational and lived as if the material and absolute did not matter. Staying exclusively in the lower right part of the matrix can be just as misleading, limiting and stultifying as confining one's vision to the upper left. The only strategy that really works is to keep the tension moving dialectically across all positions in the matrix. This is what allows us to better understand how relational meanings (such as value) are internalized in material things, events and practices (such as concrete labor processes) constructed in absolute space and time. We can, to take another example, debate interminably all manner of ideas and designs expressive of the relationality of Ground Zero, but at some point something has to be materialized in absolute space and time. Once built, the site acquires a "permanence" (Whitehead's term) of physical form. And while it is always open to reconceptualize the meaning of that material form so that people can learn to live it differently, the sheer materiality of construction in absolute space and time carries its own weight and authority. By the same token, political movements that aspire to exercise some power in the world remain ineffectual until they assert a material presence. It is all fine and good, for example, to evoke relational conceptions such as the proletariat in motion or the multitude rising up. But no one knows what any of that means until real bodies go into the absolute spaces of the streets of Seattle, Quebec City and Genoa at a particular moment in absolute time. Rights, Don Mitchell perceptively observes, mean nothing without the ability to concretize them in absolute space and time:

If the right to the city is a cry and a demand, then it is only a cry that is heard and a demand that has force to the degree that there is a space from and within which this cry and demand is visible. In public space – on street corners or in parks, in the streets during riots and demonstrations – political organizations can represent them-selves to a larger population and through this representation give their cries and demands some force. By claiming space in public, by creating public spaces, social groups themselves become public.

Public space, Mitchell correctly insists, "is material" and it "constitutes an actual site, a place, a ground within which and from which political activity flows."[23] It is only when relationality connects to the absolute spaces and times of social and material life that politics comes alive. To neglect that connectivity is to court political irrelevance.

Gaining some sense of how space is and how different spatialities and spatio-temporalities work is crucial to the construction of a distinctively geographical imagination. But space turns out to be an extraordinarily complicated key word. It functions as a compound word and has multiple determinations such that no one of its particular meanings can properly be understood in isolation from all the others. But that is precisely what makes the term, particularly when conjoined with time, so rich in possibilities.

23. D. Mitchell, *The Right to the City: Social Justice and the Fight for Public Space* (New York: The Guilford Press, 2003) pp. 129–352.

INDEX